HOME OFFICE RESEARCH STUDY

# Public Interest Case Assessment Schemes

by Debbie Crisp, Claire Whittaker and Jessica Harris

A HOME OFFICE
RESEARCH AND PLANNING UNIT
REPORT

LONDON: HMSO

© *Crown copyright 1995*
*Applications for reproduction should be made to HMSO*

ISBN 0 11 341139 1

HOME OFFICE RESEARCH STUDIES

'Home Office Research Studies' comprise reports on research undertaken in the Home Office to assist in the exercise of its administrative functions, and for the information of the judicature, the services for which the Home Secretary has responsibility (direct or indirect) and the general public.

On the last pages of this report are listed titles already published in this series, in the preceding series *Studies in the Causes of Delinquency and the Treatment of Offenders,* and in the series of *Research and Planning Unit Papers.*

**HMSO**

Standing order service

Placing an order with HMSO BOOKS enables a customer to receive other titles in this series automatically as published.

This saves time, trouble and expense of placing individual orders and avoids the problem of knowing when to do so.

For details please write to HMSO BOOKS (PC11B.2), Publications Centre, P.O. Box 276, London SW8 5DT and quoting reference 25.08.011.

The standing order service also enables customers to receive automatically as published all material of their choice which additionally saves extensive catalogue research. The scope and selectivity of the service has been extended by new techniques, and there are more than 3,500 classifications to choose from. A special leaflet describing the service in more detail may be obtained on request.

# Foreword

A major function of the Crown Prosecution Service is to assess whether the public interest will be served by taking a case to court. The criteria which crown prosecutors should apply in arriving at a decision are set out in the Code for Crown Prosecutors, but in order to apply them effectively crown prosecutors need to have reliable and objective information about offenders.

The probation service first expressed concern about gaps in the information available to prosecutors in 1986, at about the time the CPS was set up, and initiated an experimental Public Interest Case Assessment (PICA) scheme in Inner London. The results were sufficiently encouraging for further schemes to be developed in three other probation areas. The schemes were evaluated by the Home Office Research and Planning Unit in order to provide firm evidence of what the schemes achieved and at what cost. This report summarises the findings of the evaluation.

Roger Tarling
*Head of Research and Planning Unit*

# Acknowledgements

This project depended on the work and commitment of the PICA probation officers, and on that of their support staff and management. We are especially grateful to Chris Mitchell and Sally Lewis, who were the national co-ordinators for the schemes, Amanda Brown, Harry Matthews and Julie Scarsbrook from the Inner London Probation Service, Keith Young and and Janice Matthews in the West Midlands, John Heaton and Larry O'Grady from Greater Manchester and Dave Murray in Northumbria. Special thanks are also due to the ILPS staff who input all the probation monitoring data. In addition we are indebted to CPS staff, both at Headquarters and in the branches, whose co-operation was vital to the project.

Many Home Office colleagues helped with the project, and particular thanks to Anna Meadow, Steph McGuiness, Vikki D'Amore, Zoë James and Paul Goodrich who assisted with data collection and analysis, and to Simon Field who provided much of the data for the cost-benefit analysis.

DEBBIE CRISP

CLAIRE WHITTAKER

JESSICA HARRIS

# Contents

|  | Page |
|---|---|
| Foreword | iii |
| Acknowledgements | iv |
| Summary | vii |
| **Chapter 1** Introduction | 1 |
| **Chapter 2** Operation of the PICA schemes | 7 |
| **Chapter 3** The outcomes of cases registered by the PICA schemes | 17 |
| **Chapter 4** Cost-effectiveness of PICA schemes | 25 |
| **Chapter 5** Discussion | 31 |
| **Appendix A** List of offences for PICA | 35 |
| **Appendix B** Examples of PICA reports from the pilot areas | 37 |

PUBLIC INTEREST CASE ASSESSMENT SCHEMES

# Summary

When the Crown Prosecution Service was set up criteria were drawn up which crown prosecutors were required to apply when deciding whether a case should go to court. These criteria included a number of public interest considerations, and after a time it became apparent that relevant information about defendants was not always available to the CPS. The probation service, initially in Inner London, sought to fill some of the information gaps by providing reports based on interviews with defendants in selected cases. The Public Interest Case Assessment (PICA) scheme pioneered in London was later extended to three more areas, namely Greater Manchester, Northumbria and the West Midlands, to assess whether it was worth employing probation officers to improve the scope and quality of information available to prosecutors. The Royal Commission on Criminal Justice recommended the extension of PICA to other areas if the Home Office evaluation showed it to be worthwhile: this study presents the results.

The schemes were confined to a range of common offences, namely theft, public order (including being drunk and disorderly) and criminal damage. During the period of the evaluation cases falling within these offence categories were screened for possible inclusion in the PICA scheme. Some were ruled out because the defendant's criminal history made him or her an unlikely candidate for discontinuance, and serious theft cases were also excluded although the precise criteria which determined what cases were registered varied somewhat between areas. A total of 3,123 cases were initially registered by the PICA schemes, and these defendants were written to by the probation service. The consent and co-operation of those written to was required for a PICA interview to take place, and 1,124 defendants were interviewed. In terms of weekly throughput, the number of cases registered in an average week for the four schemes ranged from 12 to 19, and the average number of interviews ranged from two to eight.

A report was prepared only where the interview uncovered verifiable information which would be relevant to the decision as to whether prosecution would be in the public interest. In all, 62 per cent of interviews resulted in a report, amounting to a total of 741 reports.

**Main aims**

The central aims of the study were:

i. to measure the cost-effectiveness of the schemes;

ii. to measure any change in public interest discontinuances as a result of PICA;

iii. to assess whether the schemes provided relevant information to which prosecutors would not otherwise have had access.

# PUBLIC INTEREST CASE ASSESSMENT SCHEMES

**Main findings**

i. Savings to criminal justice agencies arising from discontinuance of cases where it was decided as a result of a PICA report that prosecution would be inappropriate covered only about one-fifth of the costs of the schemes. There were, however, substantial differences in cost-effectiveness between areas: it was estimated that the savings achieved covered between 10 per cent and 29 per cent of their costs.

ii. Discontinuance rates for those on whom a report was prepared was 27 per cent – more than double the rate for those who did not respond to the approach from the PICA team. A substantial number of cases in which crown prosecutors judged that it would have been inappropriate to prosecute were therefore diverted from the court process.

iii. In all the areas the CPS said that the PICA reports provided new information in around three-quarters of cases, although in most instances the report did not alter the initial decision to prosecute. However, where a case was discontinued the contribution which the report made to the decision was considered to have been 'crucial' in 53 per cent and 'helpful' in 42 per cent of cases.

The study obtained a wide range of information about the factors associated with discontinuance and some of the subsidiary effects of PICA.

- In cases which were terminated following provision of a PICA report, between 71 per cent and 94 per cent of discontinuances in the four areas were on public interest grounds. By contrast, other research has shown that public interest reasons account for only about one-third of all CPS discontinuances.

- Older offenders were more likely than younger offenders to get in touch with PICA officers, with a particularly low response from those aged under 18 who were less than half as likely to respond to an approach from the PICA team.

- Where cases went to court, those which had been subject to a PICA report were much more likely to result in a discharge than cases in which there was no interview. This suggests that PICA was accurately targeting cases where discontinuance appeared to be a realistic option, but it leaves open the question of why so many cases where a PICA report was provided went to court where the eventual penalty was nominal.

- In addition to providing reports, PICA officers often provided support for those they interviewed. In most cases they gave advice on court matters, and help with personal matters was also common – those with no previous experience of the courts were likely to be particularly anxious about the case and ignorant about procedures. This suggests that other ways of providing basic information of this type could be explored.

When interviewed, crown prosecutors almost always expressed their appreciation of the scheme. Sometimes it caused them to alter their initial view of a case; at others it made them more confident that their initial decision (usually to proceed with the case) was right.

# SUMMARY

Both probation officers and crown prosecutors felt that they had benefited from inter-agency working, which gave each a better understanding of the other. Defendants often expressed their appreciation for the trouble probation officers took to explain to them how the process would operate, and sometimes to help them tackle personal problems.

In sum, the schemes succeeded in so far as their aim was to provide information which improved the quality of CPS decision-making and avoided the financial and human costs which result when cases are taken to court unnecessarily. They also enabled the probation service to meet a need for support for people who were finding it difficult to cope with the stress or practical difficulties of being caught up in the criminal process. There was, however, a substantial net financial cost, with the probation resources needed for the schemes outweighing the savings made by diverting cases from court in all areas. Since the financial gap was so wide, it seems unlikely that the extension of PICA would be seen as worthwhile. However, some of the gaps in information which the study identified could perhaps be filled in other ways, bearing in mind the range of pre-trial services which have been built up in recent years.

PUBLIC INTEREST CASE ASSESSMENT SCHEMES

# 1 Introduction

One of the main aims of the Crown Prosecution Service, set up in 1986, was to provide effective, independent screening of cases so that only appropriate cases reach court. Detailed criteria which crown prosecutors should apply when deciding whether a case should be pursued are set out under two main headings in the Code for Crown Prosecutors. First, the case should be dropped if there is insufficient evidence to guarantee "a reasonable prospect of conviction"; and second, if there is sufficient evidence, the prosecutor should determine whether prosecution is in the public interest. In order to implement the public interest criteria properly, crown prosecutors need information about the offender as well as the offence. While the police are usually the sole source of information about the offence, there may be gaps in the information they are able to provide about the offender. The Public Interest Case Assessment (PICA) schemes were a joint initiative between the CPS and the probation service to assess the possible role of the probation service in plugging these gaps. They were a development of a pioneering scheme set up by the Inner London Probation Service (ILPS) in 1988 (Stone 1990).

In the absence of PICA schemes the CPS is, in most cases, dependent on the police for information about defendants' personal circumstances which may be relevant to the decision as to whether prosecution is in the public interest. Whilst the police do focus on personal details as well as the offence (as they are bound to do when deciding whether to caution) they cannot be expected always to extract as much information about a defendant as can be achieved by a probation officer through a lengthy interview. Even if the police gave details about defendants still higher priority, difficulties could remain: in relation to the original ILPS scheme Stone (1990) commented that defendants may be unwilling to disclose "personal and potentially embarrassing information to those who had just arrested them". In practice, although there is nothing to stop prosecutors considering relevant details from other sources, previous research has shown that they only infrequently receive information beyond that provided by the police (Crisp and Moxon 1994). Details do occasionally come to CPS attention via the defence solicitor, but this does not happen systematically and the information may be unverified. A further major limitation of relying on the defence is that in the kinds of minor cases which are the strongest candidates for public interest discontinuance, defendants are often unrepresented.

The Royal Commission on Criminal Justice discussed the PICA schemes, and commented on the basis of early results that:

# PUBLIC INTEREST CASE ASSESSMENT SCHEMES

> ... it is likely that expansion of PICA across the country would lead to significant benefits. We recognise that there are resource implications but we would expect these to be offset at least to some extent by the saving in court time and otherwise resulting from the identification of cases which did not have to be prosecuted.... Subject to [the Home Office evaluation] we recommend that the scheme be put on a formal and systematic basis and extended as far as practicable across the country. (Chapter 5 para 61.)

**The origins of PICA**

In March 1986 the Association of Chief Officers of Probation produced a paper entitled 'Diversion from Custody and Prosecution' which identified the potential gap in information available to crown prosecutors and proposed the creation of a scheme whereby the probation service would furnish the CPS with details about a defendant's personal circumstances to aid their public interest review. It was proposed that PICA schemes should provide the CPS with:

> ... sound, verified and relevant information describing a defendant's personal circumstances which could assist the Crown Prosecutors to reach an informed decision as to the merits of discontinuing a case on public interest grounds (ILPS, 1991).

To this end the Vera Institute of Justice,[1] in conjunction with the CPS and the probation service, was commissioned to design and evaluate an experimental PICA project at an Inner London magistrates' court. The experiment ran for six months at Horseferry Road Magistrates' Court, and focused on defendants charged with theft or criminal damage, or under sections 4 or 5 of the Public Order Act 1985 (which deal with threatening behaviour and disorderly behaviour respectively). The offence of being drunk and disorderly was also included (under the public interest heading). Defendants were excluded if they were already on bail for other matters, or if in addition to an offence covered by the PICA scheme they had been charged with a more serious offence which did not come within the scope of the scheme. At the same time, previous convictions or cautions were not necessarily seen as a bar.

The project randomly allocated cases falling within the target population to an experimental group and a control group. A total of 141 defendants within the experimental group agreed to be interviewed, and in 112 cases relevant and verifiable information about defendants' personal circumstances were discovered and a PICA report written. The rate of public interest discontinuances for the target population prior to the experiment was only one per cent; during the course of the project this increased to seven per cent for the experimental group. The rate also increased (to four per cent) for the control group. Stone (1990) referred to this as the 'halo effect' whereby the existence of the project increases the number of cases dropped generally, not just for those falling within the scheme, because it concentrates minds more generally on the need to consider the option of discontinuance.

Although the numbers involved were relatively small, the project's findings were well received and attracted a great deal of interest both within the probation service and from other criminal justice agencies. As a result a PICA scheme, closely based on the Vera

---

[1] The Vera Institute of Justice is a New York-based non-profit making organisation that works with government to improve the quality of public services in criminal justice fields.

# INTRODUCTION

experiment, was established on a more permanent basis in Inner London in March 1990. The first annual report of the Inner London scheme was encouraging, and in the autumn of 1991 PICA was extended to include three new schemes. The probation areas involved were Greater Manchester, Northumbria and the West Midlands. These schemes, together with the ILPS project, have been described briefly in earlier reports (see Brown and Crisp, 1992; Inner London Probation Service 1991, 1992 and 1993).

**The operation of the schemes**

The way in which the schemes operated broadly replicated the ILPS scheme. The arrangement in most areas was that each day a member of the probation PICA team would go through the police files received at local CPS offices and collect copies of the initial police prosecution reports on alleged offenders falling within the target group – details of the target offences were very similar to those for the Vera experiment and are set out in Appendix A. A letter would then be sent to defendants outlining the nature of PICA, and inviting them to participate. The letter stressed the voluntary nature of the project, that no information would be collected without the defendant's agreement, and that only with their consent would a copy of any resulting report be sent to the CPS. It was also made clear that copies of the report would be sent to the defence and the police.

Defendants contacting the schemes were offered an interview if there was sufficient time for a report to be prepared before their next court appearance, and if they had not already entered a plea. Those who decided to participate were asked to sign a form indicating that they understood the nature of the scheme and that they had agreed to take part. They would then be interviewed by a probation officer.

Not all defendants who initially responded in the end chose to participate; and not all interviews yielded details relating to the defendant's personal situation which were germane or verifiable. However, where the interview provided relevant information a report would be prepared and submitted to the CPS. Reports concentrated on the defendant's circumstances, drawing on sources such as employers, doctors or any relevant documentation for verification – they did not discuss the alleged offence, or contain any recommendations for sentence. Examples of PICA reports from all areas, selected on the basis that they were typical of such reports, are in Appendix B.

During the Vera experiment, two-thirds of the reports reached prosecutors before the defendant's first court appearance. In the first year of the ILPS project which succeeded the initial experiment, the PICA team was able to supply the report to the CPS prior to the first court date in 90 per cent of cases.

Although there were some differences in the way the schemes operated in each area (as described in Chapter 2) the operation was broadly similar. Figure 1 shows how PICA was designed to fit into the prosecution process. Wherever possible, reports were prepared prior to first court appearance so that if a defendant were to be diverted from the prosecution process this would happen as early as practicable. Early diversion maximises the cost savings for all agencies involved in the proceedings, and minimises avoidable anxiety and distress for both defendants and potential witnesses.

# PUBLIC INTEREST CASE ASSESSMENT SCHEMES

**Figure 1: Flow chart of prosecution process**

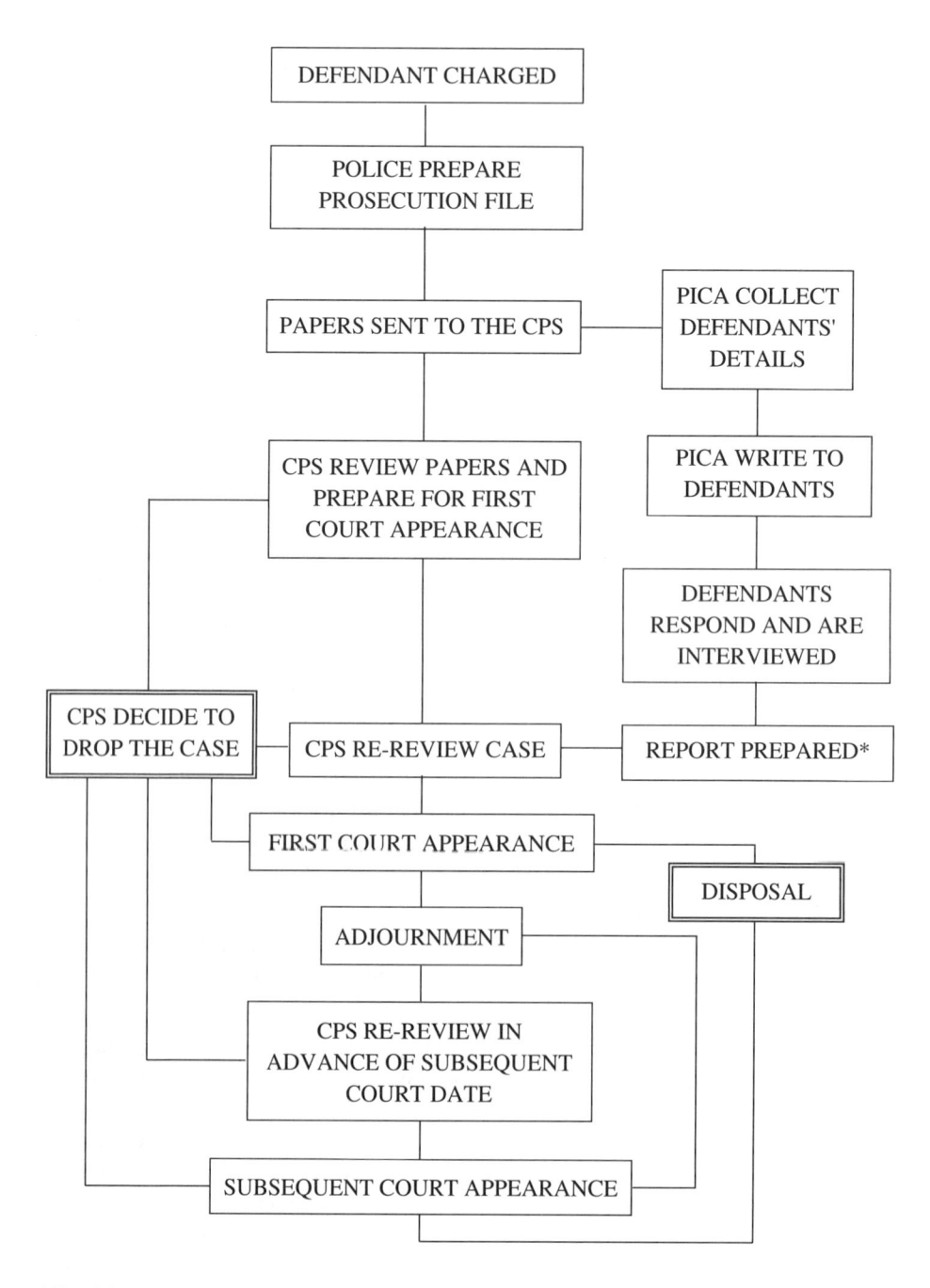

```
                    ┌─────────────────────┐
                    │ DEFENDANT CHARGED   │
                    └──────────┬──────────┘
                               │
                    ┌──────────┴──────────┐
                    │  POLICE PREPARE     │
                    │  PROSECUTION FILE   │
                    └──────────┬──────────┘
                               │
                    ┌──────────┴──────────┐     ┌─────────────────┐
                    │ PAPERS SENT TO THE  ├─────┤ PICA COLLECT    │
                    │        CPS          │     │ DEFENDANTS'     │
                    └──────────┬──────────┘     │ DETAILS         │
                               │                └────────┬────────┘
                    ┌──────────┴──────────┐     ┌────────┴────────┐
                    │ CPS REVIEW PAPERS   │     │ PICA WRITE TO   │
                    │ AND PREPARE FOR     │     │ DEFENDANTS      │
                    │ FIRST COURT         │     └────────┬────────┘
                    │ APPEARANCE          │              │
                    └──────────┬──────────┘     ┌────────┴────────┐
                               │                │ DEFENDANTS      │
  ┌──────────────┐             │                │ RESPOND AND ARE │
  │ CPS DECIDE TO│             │                │ INTERVIEWED     │
  │ DROP THE CASE├──┬──────────┴──────────┐     └────────┬────────┘
  └──────┬───────┘  │ CPS RE-REVIEW CASE  ├──────────────┤
         │          └──────────┬──────────┘     ┌────────┴────────┐
         │                     │                │ REPORT PREPARED*│
         │          ┌──────────┴──────────┐     └─────────────────┘
         │          │ FIRST COURT         │
         │          │ APPEARANCE          ├─────┐
         │          └──────────┬──────────┘     │
         │                     │          ┌─────┴─────┐
         │          ┌──────────┴──────────┐│ DISPOSAL │
         │          │ ADJOURNMENT         │└───────────┘
         │          └──────────┬──────────┘
         │                     │
         │          ┌──────────┴──────────┐
         │          │ CPS RE-REVIEW IN    │
         │          │ ADVANCE OF          │
         │          │ SUBSEQUENT          │
         │          │ COURT DATE          │
         │          └──────────┬──────────┘
         │                     │
         └──────────┬──────────┴──────────┐
                    │ SUBSEQUENT COURT    │
                    │ APPEARANCE          │
                    └─────────────────────┘
```

* The majority, but not all, reports are prepared in time for first court appearance.

# INTRODUCTION

**Aims of the Research**

The main aims of the study were:

- to examine whether PICA schemes were successful in providing relevant and reliable information which would not otherwise have been available to the CPS;
- to assess whether or not the rate at which cases were dropped on public interest grounds was affected by the existence of PICA;
- to examine the degree and type of contact which probation officers had with individual defendants as part of the scheme, and how useful this contact was judged to be;
- to assess whether the PICA schemes were cost-effective

**Methodology**

The schemes were monitored for a 12-month period from the Autumn of 1991 to 1992. Each of the schemes recorded a limited amount of information about defendants invited to participate in each project in a PICA register (age, sex, offence, date of first court appearance, final disposal etc.) Probation officers also completed a much more detailed monitoring form for all defendants who agreed to be interviewed, whether or not a PICA report was then submitted to the CPS. This gave details of the defendant's personal circumstances revealed at interview – for example whether the defendant was in employment, receiving treatment from a doctor, in financial difficulty etc. – And gave some indication of the contents of any resulting PICA report. For those on whom a report was submitted to the CPS, prosecutors recorded whether, on first looking at the report, they decided to proceed with the case and, more generally, whether they found the report helpful. In cases which were dropped on public interest grounds, prosecutors indicated the reasons for their decision, and the extent to which they were influenced by the PICA report.

Cases where the defendant was registered by the PICA schemes but for whatever reason did not take part in the project served as the main basis for comparison with cases where the defendant was interviewed. A limitation of using for comparison those defendants who chose not to become involved with PICA is that they may have had good reasons for not contacting the scheme (for example they may have had a long history of offending and have assessed the chances that the case against them would be dropped as remote). However, since the reasons why defendants' declined to participate is not known, it is not possible to assess how far the sample is biased as a result.

To supplement the information from cases where no interview was carried out, a pre-pilot monitoring exercise was undertaken in the three areas where new PICA schemes were established. Prosecutors tracked defendants falling within the PICA target group for about one month to give some indication of the rate at which cases were dropped. This was intended to show whether pilot areas experienced the 'halo effect' identified by Stone (above), whereby the discontinuance rate for cases falling outside the PICA scheme also increased.

# PUBLIC INTEREST CASE ASSESSMENT SCHEMES

To complement the statistical data, prosecutors and probation officers who were to some degree involved with the schemes were interviewed. In all, 15 probation staff were interviewed (including the two national co-ordinators and two Assistant Chief Probation Officers) and 10 Branch, Assistant Branch and Senior Crown Prosecutors (including the officer at Headquarters with oversight of the project). Since the number of reports seen by individual prosecutors in each area were not large, discussion groups were held to get a more rounded view of how the schemes had affected day-to-day business. The issues raised at interview and in the discussion groups were whether PICA was felt to be effective, what were seen as the advantages and disadvantages of the scheme, and whether any improvements could be made to current practice. In addition, regular visits were made to each of the schemes and researchers frequently sat in on meetings and seminars for PICA and CPS staff.

**Structure of the report**

The way the schemes operated, including the targeting of cases for inclusion and the characteristics of defendants are discussed in Chapter 2. Chapter 3 deals with the outcomes of cases, including changes in discontinuance rates following the introduction of PICA and reasons given for discontinuance. Chapter 4 provides estimates of the financial costs and benefits of PICA, and the findings are discussed in Chapter 5.

# 2 Operation of the PICA schemes

**Targeting cases**

Although the scheme pioneered in Inner London provided the blueprint for the schemes developed elsewhere, there were some differences in the way they were organised and the way in which they targeted defendants for inclusion. The differences both in the schemes themselves and in the kinds of individuals they dealt with are described in this chapter. The information about the schemes draws on interviews with those involved, and material produced by the individual probation areas describing the schemes.

The scope of the PICA interviews was the same everywhere, concentrating on the defendant's domestic situation, health matters, financial circumstances and any contact they had had with other agencies. Other matters which were felt to be relevant to public interest considerations were also covered, but probation officers were precluded from discussing the offence itself. The specific criteria in the Code which PICA focused on were:

- the youth of the defendant, where the stigma of a conviction could cause irreparable harm to the future prospects of the individual;

- old age or infirmity, where the pre-1994 code stated that the crown prosecutor "should be reluctant to prosecute unless there is a real possibility of repetition or the offence is of such gravity that it is impossible to overlook";

- mental disorder, where discontinuance may be appropriate unless the wider public interest (for example because the offence is serious) calls for prosecution.[1] The pre-1994 Code made it clear that if the probable effect of a prosecution outweighs the interests of justice, a prosecutor should discontinue a case.

The Code also calls on crown prosecutors to consider whether a nominal penalty is the likely outcome, in which case the length and cost of proceedings should be taken into account. This begs the question of why a nominal penalty is likely, as this will depend on offence details and public interest factors that fall outside PICA as well as the kind of personal information which PICA provided.

Interviews did not cover all the public interest criteria in the Code – some would have been known from other sources, whilst those to do with the offence were specifically excluded from PICA. Thus staleness of the offence, a change in the victim's attitude (i.e. where the victim later expresses a wish that no further action be taken), or the fact that the defendant was only "on the fringe of the action" were not seen as appropriate to PICA.

---

[1] The CPS revised their Code early in 1992 to take account of Home Office Circular 66/90 which, among other things, sets out criteria to be applied when deciding how to deal with mentally disordered defendants.

# PUBLIC INTEREST CASE ASSESSMENT SCHEMES

**Provision of PICA reports**

Where the probation officer uncovered information at interview which he or she believed was relevant to the decision to discontinue a case and where information was verifiable, a report was submitted to the CPS. Figure 2 shows the number of cases registered by the PICA schemes during the evaluation period, the number of interviews undertaken, and reports written. It can be seen that in all the areas less than half the defendants who were registered with the scheme were interviewed. In most cases this was because the defendant failed to respond, but in some instances no interview took place either because there was insufficient time or because the defendant withdrew or failed to keep an appointment.

There were large differences in the extent to which PICA officers wrote reports following interviews. In Coventry a report was written in almost all cases, and in Inner London reports were written in about 80 per cent. By contrast, in Oldham and Newcastle reports were written on less than half of defendants who were interviewed. Some of the differences arose from the way cases were targeted in the four areas – i.e. with more cases eliminated without any approach being made to the defendant in Coventry and London because their criminal history meant that it was very unlikely that they would be seen as candidates for discontinuance. The descriptions which follow give some feel for the differences between the four schemes.

**Figure 2 Throughput of PICA schemes**

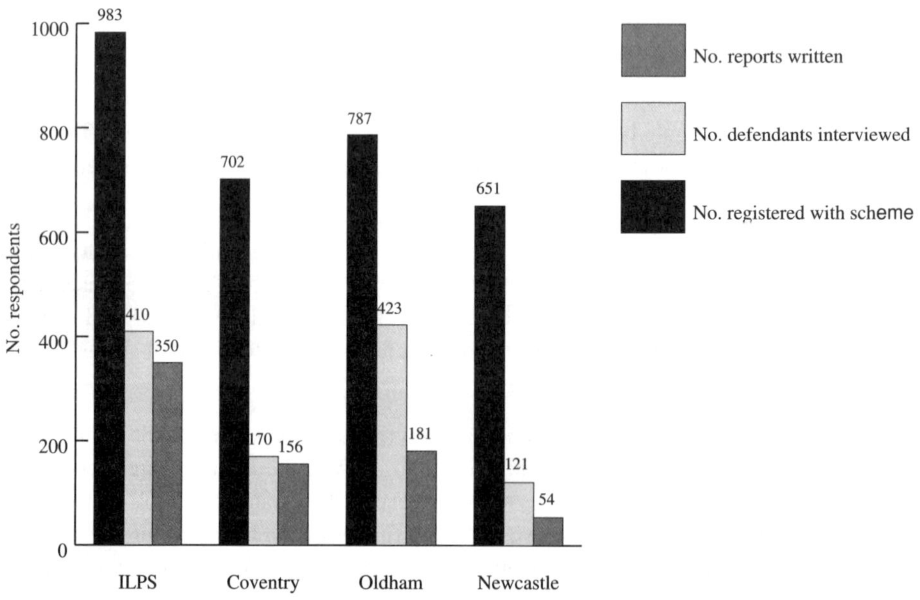

# OPERATION OF THE PICA SCHEMES

*Inner London*

The ILPS scheme was the most established of those examined; it had been in operation for some 18 months before the other schemes came into being. It was also the largest. The PICA team serviced three Inner London Magistrates' courts: Horseferry Road (where the Vera experiment took place), Marylebone Road and Great Marlborough Street. The project was staffed by a full-time senior probation officer and two full-time main grade probation officers. Support staff were shared with the bail information scheme. Each morning, copies of the file papers received by the CPS in respect of defendants falling within the PICA target group would be forwarded to the probation officers (see Appendix A for offences included). These papers would then be reviewed jointly by the two probation officers assigned to PICA and also by the Senior Probation Officer.

A degree of filtering would be introduced at this stage: for example, defendants might not be contacted where there was either a long list of previous convictions, or recent convictions for similar offences; cases where there was clear evidence of premeditation were liable to be excluded, as were cases where the value of property involved was high (although there was not a fixed limit as other factors might tip the balance where inclusion based on value alone was marginal). Where a defendant failed to respond to the initial contact letter, a follow-up letter would be sent if time allowed. Defendants would not generally be contacted where there were less than six days before their next court appearance. Although some defendants falling within the target group lived well away from Central London this was not seen as a bar to participation in PICA: it was felt that if people were able to travel to London where the alleged offence took place, they would not necessarily be deterred from making the same journey for an interview.

*West Midlands*

The West Midlands scheme was established in September 1991. It serviced Coventry Magistrates' Court (and was extended to Solihull after the evaluation period ended). It was staffed by two full-time main grade probation officers and one full-time assistant. The team was managed by a senior probation officer who also had responsibility for the local bail information schemes. When PICA first came into operation it was based in probation offices at the local court complex, but during the first year it moved to share offices with the bail information team which was felt to provide a less intimidating venue for interviews. In the early stages of the scheme the probation officers would take turns in collecting the details on PICA defendants from the nearby CPS offices, which meant that they became known to CPS staff and gained useful informal feedback.

The Coventry scheme operated to a much tighter timetable than the others, with the first court appearance usually scheduled for about a week after the probation officer first saw the file. Any reports therefore had to be produced very quickly if they were to reach the CPS in advance of first hearing. It also meant that if a case were to be dropped as a result of the report prosecutors would rarely have enough time to send out a section 23

# PUBLIC INTEREST CASE ASSESSMENT SCHEMES

discontinuance notice (which advises the defendant of the decision to drop the case in advance of the hearing). Savings would consequently have been less.

PICA staff at Coventry became aware through feedback from those they approached that the letters they sent out inviting participation were often felt to be unclear. They produced a much simplified version of the letter with the help of an expert in plain English. (For a fuller description of the West Midlands project see West Midlands Probation Service, 1993.)

*Greater Manchester*

Prior to the introduction of the PICA project in Oldham the probation service managed to negotiate a slightly longer bail period for cases falling within the PICA scheme. This meant that the two full-time PICA officers and their part-time clerical officer were better able to plan their time than staff in the other schemes. The day-to-day operation of PICA in this area differed in one important respect, in that a CPS administrative officer would undertake the initial screening of police files to identify PICA target cases. The probation officer then sent letters to all these defendants, without applying the targeting criteria employed in the Inner London and Coventry schemes. The probation officers took the view that since it was a pilot project there was scope for encompassing a wide range of cases, and consequently they registered more defendants who were unlikely to qualify for discontinuance.

*Northumbria*

The Newcastle scheme was staffed by one full-time main grade probation officer with the support of a full-time clerical assistant. The project was overseen by the Newcastle Courts Team senior probation officer, and when the scheme was first set up its offices were based in the Crown Court. The defendant response rate to the project was significantly lower than that in other areas and it was felt that one of the reasons was that the interview venue might be off-putting. The probation officer later offered interviews in offices close to where individual defendants lived, and this appeared to increase the response rate somewhat.

As can be seen from Figure 2 not only was the response rate in this scheme the lowest of the four areas, but Newcastle also seemed to have the smallest throughput of defendants falling within the target group. It is unclear why this should have been so since the CPS branch serviced a busy urban area, and it had been anticipated that as a result the scheme would have a substantial caseload. In a high proportion of relevant cases the CPS did not receive the papers from the police in time for a PICA report to be prepared prior to first court appearance. When the targeting criteria used by ILPS were applied to these defendants the numbers within the target group fell still further. From the start of 1992 a joint police/probation cautioning scheme was introduced in the area, and it is possible that some defendants who might otherwise have fallen within the PICA target group were filtered out at this earlier stage. In the first three months of operation the scheme

## OPERATION OF THE PICA SCHEMES

contacted only 35 defendants, and just four PICA reports were prepared. From March 1992 it was decided that all defendants falling within the target group should be contacted, including defendants whose first court hearing was only a day or two away. As a result the number of defendants contacted by the scheme increased. However, the response rate remained lower than elsewhere.

### Types of offences

Overall, 37 per cent of offenders registered with PICA were interviewed. Table 1 below shows the breakdown by offence type for defendants interviewed by PICA staff compared with those originally registered with the scheme but not subsequently interviewed.

**Table 1**
**Whether the defendant was interviewed by offence for each area**

|  | Interviewed | | | Not interviewed | | |
|---|---|---|---|---|---|---|
|  | Theft | Public order | Criminal damage | Theft | Public order | Criminal damage |
|  | (n=732) | (n=250) | (n=138) | (n=1305) | (n=267) | (n=341) |
| Area | % | % | % | % | % | % |
| ILPS | 80 | 11 | 9 | 82 | 9 | 9 |
| Coventry | 43 | 36 | 21 | 64 | 22 | 14 |
| Oldham | 57 | 30 | 13 | 43 | 36 | 21 |
| Newcastle | 74 | 14 | 13 | 76 | 10 | 14 |
| Total | 65 | 22 | 12 | 68 | 14 | 18 |

Overall, Table 1 shows that those charged with theft, and especially those charged with criminal damage, were less likely than people charged with public order offences to be interviewed. However, there was no consistent pattern in the extent to which defendants in different areas responded to the invitation to participate in PICA according to type of offence, and among both those interviewed and those not interviewed there were big differences in the breakdown of offences between areas. Although theft comprised the largest offence category in all the areas, proportionately fewer theft than public order and criminal damage cases were included in the schemes. Home Office data for the areas covered by the schemes showed that theft comprised between 81 per cent and 91 per cent of cases in the target offence group in the four areas, whereas public order comprised only three to six per cent and criminal damage seven to thirteen per cent. By contrast, public order cases accounted for between eleven per cent and 36 per cent of defendants interviewed, and criminal damage for between nine per cent and 21 per cent.

The fact that theft formed a smaller proportion of the PICA caseload than the overall caseload for each area probably reflects the way cases were targeted. For example, high value thefts would normally have been excluded, especially in Inner London and

# PUBLIC INTEREST CASE ASSESSMENT SCHEMES

Coventry, whereas the sum involved would rarely have been sufficiently high to exclude criminal damage. Only relatively minor public order offences (including being drunk and disorderly) qualified for inclusion, but in practice such offences make up the majority of all public order cases.

Just two per cent of defendants interviewed by a probation officer were charged with more than one offence which came within the PICA target group, and only four per cent were charged additionally with offences which fell outside the PICA target group but were not so serious as to preclude them from the scheme. (Typically these would be minor drug offences, road traffic cases or minor assault.) By contrast, 16 per cent of the defendants who chose not to participate in PICA were charged with more than one offence, which may indicate that some defendants felt (probably rightly) that the scheme would not prove relevant to them.

Where the defendant was interviewed and the offence was property-related, PICA officers were often able to record the total value of the loss or damage involved – value is clearly a key factor for crown prosecutors in determining whether the seriousness of the offence makes it unlikely that discontinuance would be in the public interest. In each of the areas, in at least 60 per cent of cases where the information was available the amount involved totalled £100 or less – and the majority of these cases related to property worth less than £50. Comparable information was not readily available for registered cases where there was no interview, but research by Hedderman and Moxon (1991) recorded that 44 per cent of the theft cases in their sample of magistrates' courts involved less than £100 which suggests that, as expected, PICA theft cases were less serious than average.

**Defendant characteristics**

There were significant differences in the defendant profiles for the four areas in terms of gender, age and employment status.

*Gender*

Among those approached, females were more likely than males to be interviewed – they made up a quarter of those interviewed but only one-fifth of those not interviewed. However, the pattern was not consistent: in Newcastle there was no difference and at Oldham males were more likely to be interviewed.

*Age*

The Code for Crown Prosecutors indicates that the youth or old age of the defendant may be relevant to decisions to prosecute. The age profiles for defendants registered for PICA are set out in Figure 3.

# OPERATION OF THE PICA SCHEMES

**Figure 3  Ages of defendants registered with the PICA schemes**

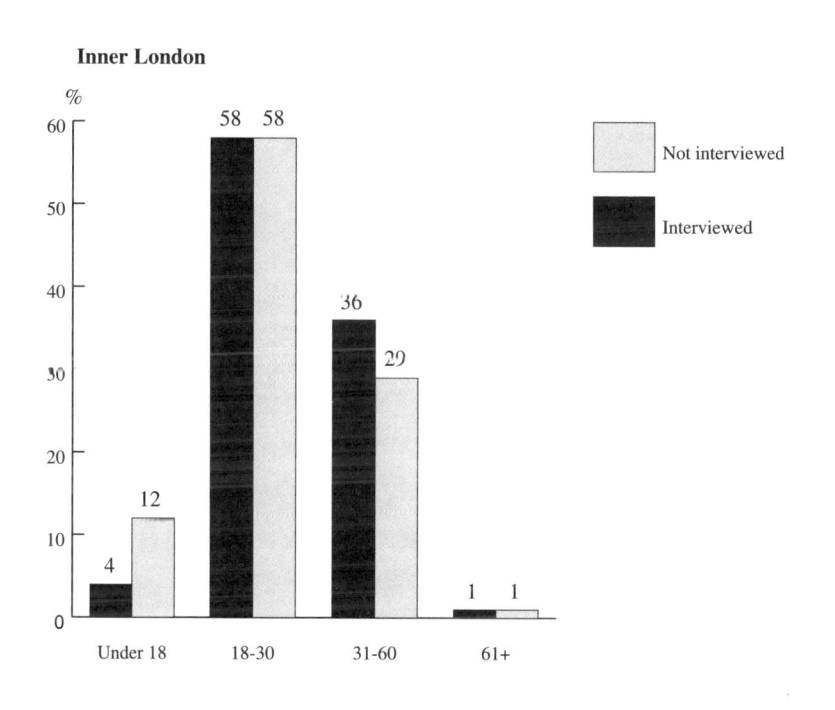

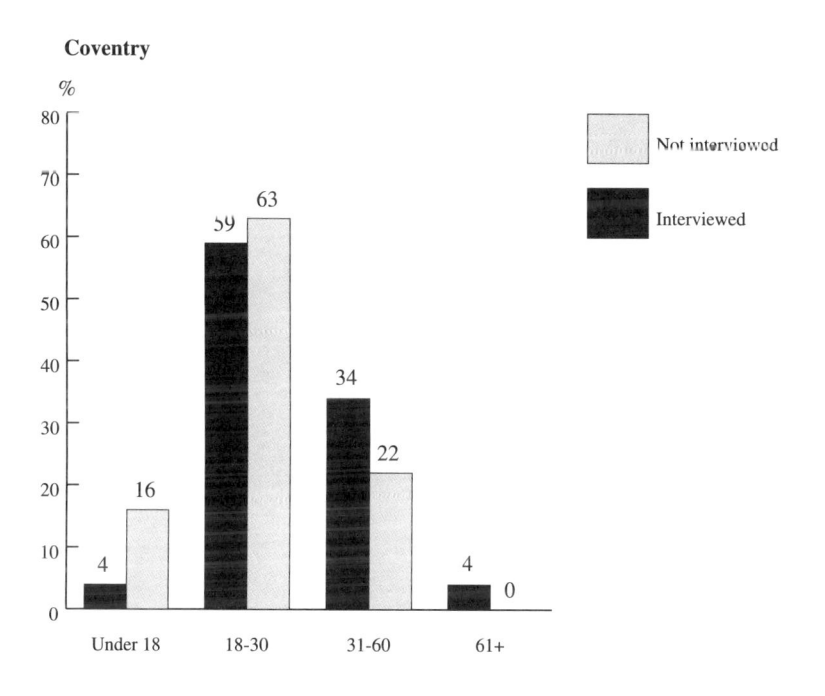

**Inner London**

| Age | Interviewed | Not interviewed |
|---|---|---|
| Under 18 | 4 | 12 |
| 18-30 | 58 | 58 |
| 31-60 | 36 | 29 |
| 61+ | 1 | 1 |

**Coventry**

| Age | Interviewed | Not interviewed |
|---|---|---|
| Under 18 | 4 | 16 |
| 18-30 | 59 | 63 |
| 31-60 | 34 | 22 |
| 61+ | 4 | 0 |

# PUBLIC INTEREST CASE ASSESSMENT SCHEMES

**Oldham**

| Age | Interviewed | Not interviewed |
|---|---|---|
| Under 18 | 8 | 14 |
| 18-30 | 67 | 64 |
| 31-60 | 23 | 23 |
| 61+ | 2 | 1 |

**Newcastle**

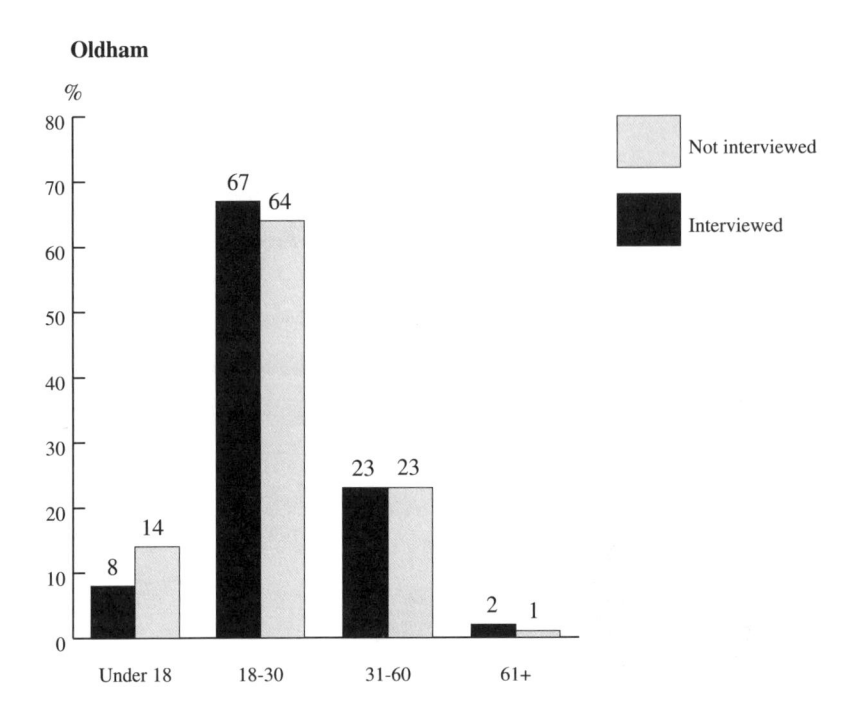

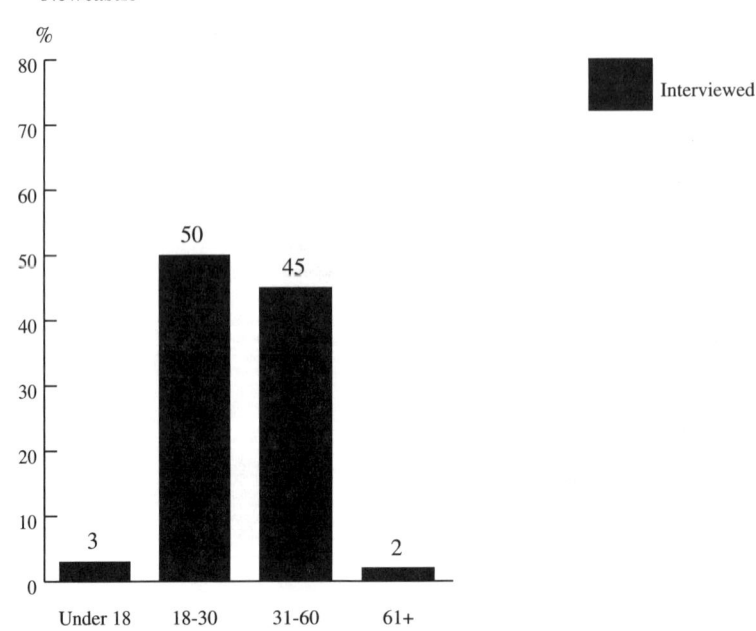

| Age | Interviewed |
|---|---|
| Under 18 | 3 |
| 18-30 | 50 |
| 31-60 | 45 |
| 61+ | 2 |

No information on the age of the defendant was available for those not interviewed at Newcastle

# OPERATION OF THE PICA SCHEMES

Figure 3 shows that in general older defendants were more likely to get in touch with a scheme. For example, the proportion of under 18-year-olds interviewed was only six per cent in the interview sample, and more than twice as high – at 14 per cent – among those not interviewed. The 18 to 30 age group were interviewed in proportion to their representation in the numbers registered in the scheme, whereas those over 30 were significantly more likely to be interviewed: in the small over 60 group, no less than 84 per cent of those contacted were interviewed.

*Ethnic origin*

Two-thirds of defendants interviewed were white and one-third non-white. It is not possible to provide a more meaningful breakdown as, at the time of the study, the probation service only collected ethnic data broken down into 'white', 'black' or 'other', and it is unclear how Asian defendants were classified. A standard classification has since been introduced to assist with monitoring in relation to Section 95 of the Criminal Justice Act 1991.

*Employment status*

In all areas less than one-third of the defendants interviewed in the PICA scheme were employed – in Newcastle the figure was one-fifth. Of those with earnings, over 70 per cent were paid less than £200 per week. (Employment details were available only for those interviewed, so no comparisons can be made with other defendants.)

*Previous criminal history*

Although the Code for Crown Prosecutors makes no *direct* mention of the influence of previous criminal history of the defendant on the public interest criteria, previous convictions can have an *indirect* impact on decisions whether to discontinue because they bear on sentence, which is more likely to be 'nominal' (and therefore to come within the Code's criteria for discontinuance) if the defendant has no previous convictions.

Overall, 55 per cent of those interviewed were first offenders. Other research suggests that this is a higher proportion of first offenders than the general run of non-motoring cases in magistrates' courts – for example, Hedderman and Moxon (1991) found that only 41 per cent of those dealt with for triable either way offences in magistrates' courts were first offenders. Interestingly, this is in line with the figures for previous convictions in areas outside London and it is only the figure for London (76 per cent) which is significantly out of line with this average.

Among those with previous convictions 26 per cent had only one prior conviction, and 66 per cent had four or less. About one in five of those with convictions had previously been given a custodial sentence. Where the nature of previous convictions was known, just over half (52 per cent) had been convicted of similar offences to those which led to their involvement with PICA. However, the majority of those with previous convictions (61 per cent) had none within the past year.

# PUBLIC INTEREST CASE ASSESSMENT SCHEMES

Defendants charged with criminal damage were more likely to have previous convictions than those accused of theft or public order offences. Defendants charged with theft from their employer were the least likely to have a criminal record. This is consistent with other research (e.g. Moxon 1988) which found that these offences tend to involve first offenders probably because those with previous convictions are less likely to be placed in a position of trust.

*Distance from scheme*

It has always been a feature of the ILPS scheme that defendants may have to travel some distance in order to be interviewed. However it was recognised that the situation in London was unusual in that the area served by the courts is a major commercial and entertainment centre to which people travel from a wide area. Defendants in the other areas lived closer to the PICA office with less than five per cent of defendants who were interviewed living outside the probation area, compared with 11 per cent of defendants who were interviewed in Inner London.

In Newcastle there was concern that defendants who lived at some distance would be deterred from attending a PICA interview. For a trial period defendants were offered travelling expenses to cover the cost of their journey to the PICA office but this did not increase the proportion of people who contacted the scheme.

**Timing**

There were big variations between areas in the extent to which reports were prepared prior to the first court appearance, ranging from 50 per cent at Newcastle, 74 per cent at Coventry and 90 per cent in Inner London and Oldham. Probation officers in Coventry were working to a much tighter timetable than those in other areas: they had less than a week in 43 per cent of cases (and rarely had more than a fortnight), whereas in Inner London and Oldham only six per cent of cases were scheduled for their first court appearance within a week of receipt of the police papers.

The differences in the time taken for case preparation should be reduced following the introduction of the new Manual of Pre-Trial Guidance for police and prosecutors which came into effect in October 1992 (towards the end of the data collection period). Under the new arrangements, there should always be at least four weeks between the date of charge and the date of first court appearance, and prosecutors should receive the police file at least two weeks prior to court.

The majority of discontinuances were made by the CPS as soon as they reviewed the case following receipt of the PICA report. However a minority in each area were made at a later stage; often this will have been for reasons unconnected with PICA, although some prosecutors felt that PICA reports could have a delayed impact in certain circumstances – for example, when taken together with other information that came to light later on.

# 3 The outcomes of cases registered by the PICA schemes

The main test of whether PICA met its aim of providing relevant information not available from other sources centred on its impact on prosecution decisions. This chapter looks first at what happened to cases which were registered for PICA, including the effect they had on discontinuance rates and reasons given where cases were dropped. The court outcomes of cases which were not discontinued are also considered.

## The impact of PICA on discontinuance rates

Figure 4 shows termination rates for each area for cases where a report was written and for those not interviewed, and also indicates the number of cases involved. Overall, 27 per cent of cases were dropped where a report was prepared compared with 13 per cent where there was no interview. In all areas the discontinuance rate was substantially higher where a report was prepared although in Newcastle this is based on very few cases, with only 13 discontinuances in all for cases involving reports.

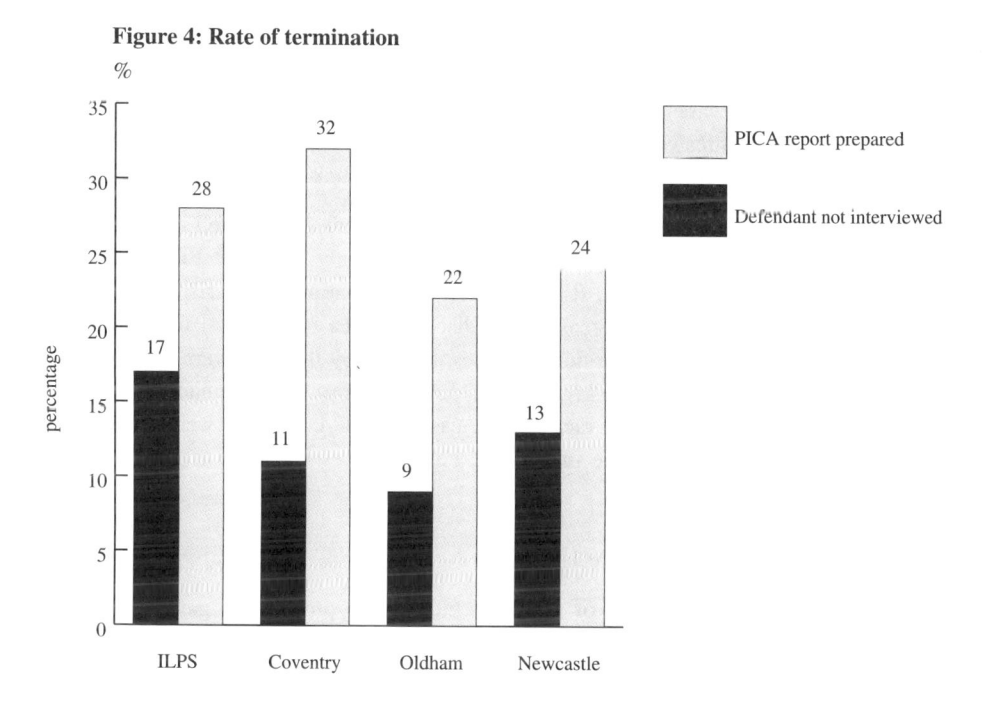

**Figure 4: Rate of termination**

| Area | Defendant not interviewed | PICA report prepared |
|---|---|---|
| ILPS | 17 | 28 |
| Coventry | 11 | 32 |
| Oldham | 9 | 22 |
| Newcastle | 13 | 24 |

# PUBLIC INTEREST CASE ASSESSMENT SCHEMES

Table 2 shows the proportion of cases discontinued where a report was written, for each of the offence categories.

**Table 2**
**Proportions of cases discontinued by offence type where a report was prepared, by area[1]**

|  | Theft | | Public order | | Criminal damage | |
|---|---|---|---|---|---|---|
|  | Report written (n=479) | No interview (n=892) | Report written (n=165) | No interview (n=247) | Report written (n=93) | No interview (n=186) |
|  | % | % | % | % | % | % |
| Inner London | 27 | 11 | 26 | 14 | 39 | 19 |
| Coventry | 38 | 8 | 17 | 2 | 38 | 14 |
| Oldham | 20 | 4 | 7 | 6 | 28 | 3 |
| Newcastle | 23 | 10 | 0 | 8 | 60 | 21 |
| *Overall* | *27* | *13* | *21* | *9* | *40* | *19* |

It can be seen from Table 2 that there was a higher - often much higher - discontinuance rate where a PICA report was provided. For example, theft cases in which there was a report were roughly twice as likely to be discontinued in London, Oldham and Newcastle than where there was no interview, and in Coventry there was a four to one difference.

In all the areas criminal damage cases were discontinued at a higher rate than other offences while theft cases were least likely to be discontinued. In public order cases a section 4 offence (threatening behaviour) was less likely to be dropped than either a section 5 offence (disorderly behaviour) or one of being drunk and disorderly.

More than three-quarters of cases (77 per cent) which were dropped following a PICA report were terminated on public interest grounds, with only 23 per cent terminated on evidential grounds. By contrast, RPU research on discontinuance (Crisp and Moxon 1994) and a CPS survey of the reasons for discontinuance (CPS 1994) found that for offences as a whole roughly one-third of cases dropped by the CPS were discontinued on public interest grounds. The high rate of public interest discontinuances in PICA cases no doubt reflects both the fact that the cases in PICA schemes were those most likely to be suitable for public interest discontinuances and the influence of the report itself.

**Factors affecting prosecution decisions**

Table 3 summarises the reason or reasons which crown prosecutors gave when they discontinued cases on public interest grounds in those cases where a report had been provided. In many instances the prosecution indicated that one reason for discontinuance

# THE OUTCOMES OF CASES REGISTERED BY THE PICA SCHEMES

was that a nominal penalty was likely. Since this reason is derived from other case factors, the table indicates the extent to which other factors were recorded in conjunction with 'nominal penalty likely'. In only 14 per cent of cases was the fact that a nominal penalty was the likely outcome the sole reason for discontinuance. In many cases where other reasons were given for discontinuance, the nominal penalty was also a factor. This overlap is because the Code makes it clear that in serious cases, prosecution should normally take place. Therefore the prosecutor is bound to consider the seriousness of each case and hence the likely outcome in considering whether to discontinue a case.

**Table 3**
**Reasons for discontinuance in the public interest for all PICA areas[1]**

|  | Theft | Public Order | Criminal damage | Number | Per cent overlap with nominal penalty |
| --- | --- | --- | --- | --- | --- |
|  | % | % | % | % | % |
| Nominal penalty likely | 54 | 44 | 52 | 80 | – |
| *Offence-related* |  |  |  |  |  |
| Trivial offence | 13 | 33 | 0 | 22 | 91 |
| Offence stale | 1 | 0 | 0 | 1 | 100 |
| Defendant on periphery of offence | 1 | 2 | 0 | 2 | 50 |
| Victim does not want to continue | 0 | 0 | 7 | 2 | 0 |
| Recompense made to victim | 2 | 0 | 41 | 13 | 69 |
| *Defendant-related* |  |  |  |  |  |
| Youth of defendant | 12 | 19 | 7 | 17 | 88 |
| Defendant old and/or infirm | 14 | 11 | 33 | 17 | 71 |
| Mental illness/stress | 45 | 33 | 24 | 59 | 58 |
| Other | 14 | 30 | 10 | 26 | 46 |

Note:
1. This information is only available for cases which were discontinued at the first review after the PICA report was available, which covers most instances.

Table 3 shows that the youth or age/infirmity of defendants were each factors in 17 discontinuances. However, the factor most commonly associated with the decision to discontinue was the mental state of the defendant. (No distinction was made between mental illness and stress on the forms completed by prosecutors.)

Just under half the discontinuances in theft cases were influenced by the fact that the defendant was mentally ill or suffering from stress. The mental health of the defendant was a factor in a quarter of public interest discontinuances in criminal damage cases and a third of those in public order cases. Overall, the mental health of the defendant was the second most frequently cited reason for terminating cases in the public interest and is discussed in more detail below.

There were some differences between areas in the reasons given for public interest discontinuances. For example, the mental health of the defendant was cited as a factor

## PUBLIC INTEREST CASE ASSESSMENT SCHEMES

by the CPS in 49 per cent of public interest discontinuances in Inner London compared to 35 per cent in Coventry and 26 per cent in Oldham. Although there were only ten cases discontinued on public interest grounds in Newcastle where a report was provided, in three of these the mental health of the defendant was cited as a factor. The CPS in Coventry and Inner London were also more likely to cite the nominal level of the expected penalty than the CPS in Oldham and Newcastle.

Further information relating to the mental and physical condition of the defendant was available from the probation service, which provided a more detailed breakdown of health-related issues. In PICA interviews 63 per cent of females and 37 per cent of males reported at least one health problem. Stress was the most frequently mentioned problem, discussed by just over half of the females and a quarter of males interviewed. Not all of these issues were put into the report, either because the information could not be verified or the probation officer felt that it was not relevant to the public interest criteria, or because the defendant did not want it to go into the report. The extent to which reports mentioned health issues is set out in Table 4.

**Table 4**
**Proportion of PICA reports in which medical problems or problems of addiction were reported**

|  | Females (n=211) | Males (n=530) |
|---|---|---|
|  | % | % |
| Physical health (total) | 20 | 11 |
| Alcohol abuse | 3 | 4 |
| Drug abuse | 3 | 3 |
| Gambling | 0 | 1 |
| Mental health | 3 | 3 |
| Stress | 47 | 21 |

Table 4 shows that some problem relating to the defendant's physical health was mentioned in 20 per cent of reports on females and 11 per cent of males in the sample. Stress was mentioned in 47 per cent of reports on females and 21 per cent of reports on males. Addictions – to alcohol, drugs or gambling – were mentioned in respect of six per cent of females and eight per cent of males.

**Outcomes of cases which went to court**

The outcomes of cases that went to court, both for cases where a report was prepared and for all cases where the defendant did not contact the PICA scheme, are shown in Figure 5.

# THE OUTCOMES OF CASES REGISTERED BY THE PICA SCHEMES

**Figure 5 Outcome of case which continued to court (ILPS, Coventry and Oldham)**

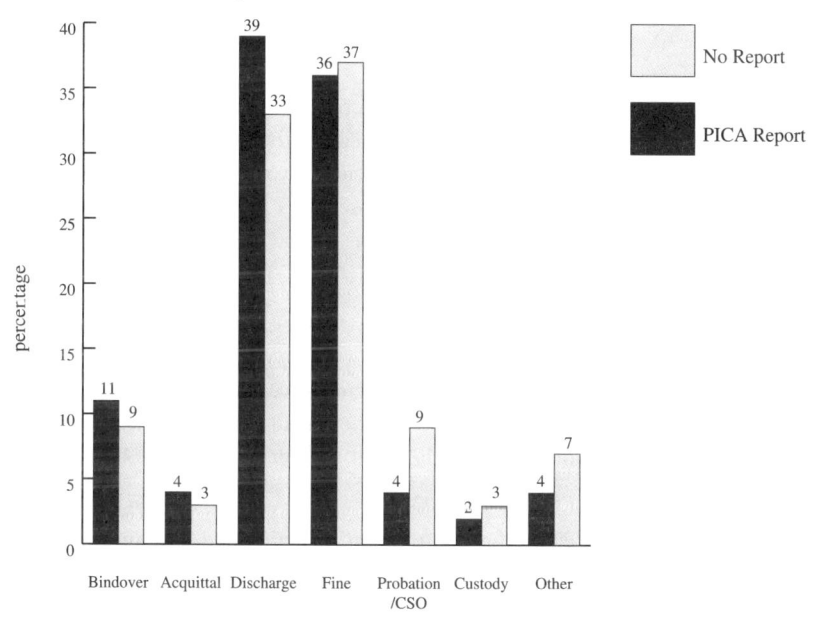

[Bar chart showing percentages for No Report vs PICA Report:
- Bindover: PICA 11, No Report 9
- Acquittal: PICA 4, No Report 3
- Discharge: PICA 39, No Report 33
- Fine: PICA 36, No Report 37
- Probation/CSO: PICA 4, No Report 9
- Custody: PICA 2, No Report 3
- Other: PICA 4, No Report 7]

In Newcastle it was not possible to follow cases where there was no report to final disposal.
Where a report was written in Newcastle:
5% resulted in a bindover, 10% aquittal, 37% discharge, 15% probation/CSO, 15% fine, 5% custody and 15% other.

It had been anticipated that sentencing for cases which had been the subject of reports, and had therefore had an extra stage of filtering compared with other cases would tend to receive more severe penalties (because more 'nominal penalty' cases would be screened out). Figure 5 shows that this expectation was not borne out: the most frequent sentences for offences in the PICA target group were fines or discharges, and it is of particular interest that cases where a report was prepared were more likely to attract a discharge. This suggests that the cases targeted for PICA are indeed strong candidates for discontinuance, and it is at first sight surprising that so many cases were taken to court and resulted in a nominal penalty despite the fact that a PICA report was provided. Part of the explanation may be that the defence had a copy of the report, and may have been able to use the material it contained to strengthen mitigation. From interviews, it was also apparent that on occasions the CPS would themselves mention mitigating factors in the PICA report, especially if the defendant was unrepresented. Further, in 14 per cent of cases where a conditional discharge was given this was not in fact the only penalty, as a compensation order was also awarded. In such cases it is possible that the interests of the victim were considered to be of overriding importance.

Few defendants eventually received a custodial sentence or more serious community penalties (probation or community service), and the figures for PICA cases are below

# PUBLIC INTEREST CASE ASSESSMENT SCHEMES

the national average for these offences which confirms the probation officers' views that PICA led them to deal with people they would not normally have seen.

*Bindovers*

Bindovers were only used in cases of public order or criminal damage. From interviews it was clear that a bindover was sometimes considered appropriate where there was a threat of recurrence, or where some record of the incident was merited but conviction would be unnecessarily heavy-handed. However, prosecutors pointed out that where a defendant is bound over there is no real saving in terms of the costs of case preparation and court time.

**Contribution of PICA in individual cases**

In all cases where a PICA report was provided prosecutors were asked to state whether the report provided them with information to which they would not otherwise have had access and, where it told them nothing new, whether it provided useful corroboration of information already on file.

In more than three-quarters of cases the PICA report had provided new information, usually about the defendant's personal circumstances, although in over 70 per cent of these cases the CPS nevertheless decided that it was in the public interest to prosecute. Where a case was dropped at the first review of the case following a PICA report, the report was judged to have been crucial to the decision in 53 per cent of cases and helpful in 42 per cent. In five per cent the report apparently played no part.

Whilst Oldham, Coventry and Inner London all said that the reports were crucial in a substantial number of cases (between 41 per cent and 60 per cent) none of the Newcastle cases were described as crucial, which is consistent with the fact that reports there had relatively little impact on discontinuance rates. In most cases where the report was not seen as crucial it was described as helpful. (All the reports in Newcastle were described simply as 'helpful'.)

**The use of unverified information**

Although the emphasis of the schemes was on *verified* information, on occasions probation officers felt it appropriate to pass on details which were thought to be relevant even if verification was not practicable – for example, in some cases where the defendant was suffering stress they had not spoken to anybody else about it, but the probation officer would be able to make his or her own judgement as to whether this had contributed to their behaviour.

The CPS were divided on the value of having unverified information in reports. Some felt that this threatened the objectivity and reliability of the information while others felt that on occasions unverified information could be worth having. As one prosecutor commented:

# THE OUTCOMES OF CASES REGISTERED BY THE PICA SCHEMES

*"[unverified information] would be helpful. Facts and figures don't add up to a picture of a person and that is what we are looking for."*

There was indirect evidence that verified information did indeed carry more weight: 38 per cent of cases where a physical health problem was mentioned in the report and confirmation obtained were discontinued compared to 25 per cent of cases where the information was included in the report but no supporting evidence was available.

**Support given to defendants**

Whilst the main aim of the PICA projects was to provide the CPS with information about defendants' personal circumstances, the nature of the work meant that in a fair proportion of cases the PICA officer would also offer the defendant advice or support. As one probation officer put it:

*"A lot of people don't realise the impact of what is happening to them - either they will go to court and think this is the same as a conviction, or have a very exaggerated idea of the outcome, thinking they'll go to prison for sure."*

There was a high level of support given to defendants on both court matters and personal matters, except at Newcastle where fewer than one-quarter of defendants received this kind of assistance. In the other three areas, between 72 per cent and 91 per cent of defendants were given advice relating to their court appearance. This was seen as particularly relevant for those who had no previous contact with the criminal justice system and who therefore had little idea of what was involved or how to obtain legal advice. Support on personal matters was given to between 41 per cent and 64 per cent of defendants in the three areas.

In order to monitor this welfare aspect of their role, PICA officers were asked to record the level of help (intensive or general) that had been given to defendants requiring support on personal matters. This varied between areas - from 28 per cent intensive support in Inner London to three per cent in Oldham. The main areas on which support was offered were coping strategies (32 per cent) and stress management (30 per cent). PICA officers were more likely to offer personal support to female defendants, which may reflect the fact that a much higher proportion were reported to be suffering from stress.

# PUBLIC INTEREST CASE ASSESSMENT SCHEMES

# 4 Cost-effectiveness of PICA schemes

An important aspect of the study was to assess the extent to which the costs incurred by the probation service in running the projects were offset by savings elsewhere in the criminal justice system. From the available data it would not be possible to make precise estimates, but a rough assessment of the cost-effectiveness of the schemes was made by comparing running costs with an approximation of the savings made where cases which would otherwise have been prosecuted were dropped as a result of PICA.

**Costs**

The annual costs of the schemes were estimated using official Home Office figures for the costs of probation staff.[1] For 1993-94, these were £31,000 for a probation officer and £18,960 for support staff. (1993-94 figures are used throughout; the relative costs and savings are likely to be similar for the period covered by the study.)

Staff costs account for most of the cost of the PICA schemes. Three out of the four schemes had two main grade officers working full time on the project with varying degrees of input from a senior probation officer and support staff. The estimated cost of a scheme with two main grade probation officers and one member of support staff is:

| | | |
|---|---|---|
| 2 POs @ £31,000 pa = | | £62,000 |
| 1 support staff @ £18,960 pa | = | £18,960 |
| TOTAL | = | £80,960 |

There will also be some cost to the Crown Prosecution Service as there are some administration duties connected with PICA - CPS staff have to put out files for probation officers, track down relevant files and inform the defendant, police and the court of decisions to discontinue. In interview, staff felt that these costs would be difficult to isolate but would be small in comparison to the cost of prosecuting the case. There would also be some cost incurred by the police where the case is referred back for a caution, but again the cost would be relatively slight.

**Cost savings**

There are potential savings for the CPS, the probation service, the prison escort service, the police as witnesses and escorts and in legal aid costs when cases are dropped. The unit costs of criminal proceedings at the magistrates' courts and the Crown Court, based mainly on the average duration of cases, have recently been estimated and the figures are set out in Table 5.

---

[1] The figures include pay, accommodation and administration costs. The probation officer category encompasses all probation officers from chief probation officer to main grade, the support staff category refers to all non-probation officer, non-ancillary staff.

# PUBLIC INTEREST CASE ASSESSMENT SCHEMES

**Table 5**
**Comparative costs of prosecutions**

| Court Proceedings | Summary | Theft |
|---|---|---|
|  | £ | £ |
| COURT SERVICE COSTS | 244 | 1018 |
| Police witnesses, escorts etc. | 18 | 117 |
| Court Service | 99 | 251 |
| Legal aid | 14 | 395 |
| CPS | 79 | 174 |
| Probation | 22 | 50 |
| Escorts | 13 | 31 |
| DISPOSAL COSTS | 11 | 251 |
| Probation service | 25 | 176 |
| Attendance centre | 1 | 2 |
| Fine | -57 | -30 |
| Imprisonment | 21 | 59 |
| Remand | 22 | 44 |
| TOTAL COSTS PER PROSECUTION | 256 | 1269 |

The overheads shown in Table 5 are calculated as an average of all cases rather than the actual cost of individual cases. For example, the legal aid overhead allows for the fact that only a proportion of cases are aided. In those cases which are legally aided, the legal aid costs will on average be three times the court proceedings costs.

The cost to the probation service under court service costs is for the preparation of pre-sentence reports and does not include costs of supervision. It has been suggested that the existence of a PICA report may reduce the amount of work involved in preparing a pre-sentence report but there was little evidence of this as PICA reports necessarily include different material to pre-sentence reports, principally because the PICA interview cannot deal with the offence. A PICA report would not, therefore, remove the need for a further interview should a pre-sentence report be called for.

Using these figures the savings in cases which were discontinued on public interest grounds because of the PICA schemes was as shown in Table 6. The figures assume that the proportion of public interest discontinuances which are attributable to PICA is equal to the difference in discontinuance rates between the cases where a PICA report was written and the control group (i.e. cases registered for PICA but where no interview was carried out).

# COST-EFFECTIVENESS OF PICA SCHEMES

## Table 6
### Savings made in cases which were discontinued on public interest grounds (£s)[1]

| PICA SCHEME | Theft[2] | Public Order | Criminal Damage[3] |
|---|---|---|---|
| | £ | £ | £ |
| Inner London | 28,952 | 221 | 630 |
| Coventry | 13,892 | 2,793 | 1,617 |
| Oldham | 10,787 | 1,205 | 1,880 |
| Newcastle | 4,855 | 0 | 316 |

Notes:
1. These estimates are based on the maximum savings if all the pre-trial work is avoided.
2. Theft prosecutions involved in PICA schemes are at the minor end of theft cases generally. Therefore the costs of theft prosecutions are estimated on the basis that the prosecutions avoided are only one third as likely to be committed for trial, and only one-third as likely to receive a custodial sentence in the Crown Court and magistrates' courts (so that less than two per cent of those sentenced would receive a custodial sentence).
3. Criminal damage cases in which the value of loss is greater than £2,000 are triable either way. All the criminal damage cases in the sample except one at Oldham were valued at less than £300. Therefore all criminal damage cases have been assumed to be summary for the purposes of this calculation.

If the annual costs of running the schemes are subtracted the following "net costs" result.

## Table 7
### Net costs to the criminal justice system from PICA schemes (£s)

| | Cost of the scheme | Savings for the system as a whole | Net costs to system as a whole | Costs covered |
|---|---|---|---|---|
| | £ | £ | £ | % |
| All PICA schemes | 304,880 | 67,148 | 237,652 | 22 |
| Inner London[1] | 102,480 | 29,803 | 72,677 | 29 |
| Coventry | 80,960 | 18,302 | 62,658 | 23 |
| Oldham[2] | 71,480 | 13,872 | 57,608 | 19 |
| Newcastle[3] | 49,960 | 5,171 | 44,789 | 10 |

Notes:
1. The Inner London scheme had one senior probation officer, two probation officers and one half-time support staff.
2. The Oldham costings take account of the fact that the scheme only had one part-time support staff.
3. The Newcastle scheme had one probation officer and one support staff.

All the schemes cost far more to run than the estimated savings. Overall, the schemes cost almost five times the maximum estimated savings to the criminal justice system. The Inner London scheme covered the highest proportion of its costs, partly because a larger total number of cases were dropped on public interest grounds, but mainly because a greater proportion of the discontinuances were theft cases which, on average, are more costly to the criminal justice system. This is mainly because a proportion of theft cases go to the Crown Court, where costs are very much higher than at magistrates' courts. In the Inner London scheme, over 80 per cent of cases which were public interest discontinuances involved theft, compared to 40 per cent in Coventry and 47 per cent in Oldham.

# PUBLIC INTEREST CASE ASSESSMENT SCHEMES

## Number of court appearances

These estimated savings assume that PICA discontinuances have no cost implications to other criminal justice agencies except the probation service. However, this is only true where cases discontinued as a result of PICA do not reach court.

In practice, more than three-quarters of discontinuances in Inner London, Coventry and Oldham were prior to or at the first court hearing. The average number of appearances for cases which were discontinued on public interest grounds were 1.6 in Inner London, 1.7 in Coventry, 1.5 in Oldham and 2.1 in Newcastle compared to an average of 1.5 appearances for all cases[2] and 3.5 for indictable cases which appeared at the magistrates' court[3]. The higher number of average appearances in Newcastle was due to the fact that the PICA report was ready for the first court appearance in only 50 per cent of cases. In Inner London and Oldham the reports were ready prior to the first appearance in 90 per cent of cases and in 74 per cent of cases in Coventry.[4]

The listing procedures at the magistrates' courts varied between areas. Justices' Clerks were asked for their views on savings in court costs where a case is discontinued at a late stage. It was felt this would often make little impact due to the numbers of cases listed to appear on any day. In some instances it could simply result in the court sitting idle for a period, particularly where a contest had been scheduled. If the maximum advantage is to be gained from dropping cases, therefore, it is essential that they are discontinued as early in the process as possible so that the court can put the time saved to good use.

## Overall changes in discontinuance rates

In addition to direct savings, the original Vera scheme (discussed in Chapter 1) indicated that PICA raised awareness of the need to focus on public interest considerations when deciding whether to proceed, and this was reflected in an increase in the discontinuance rate for cases not included in the scheme. The evaluation of all the schemes showed an increase in the discontinuance rate in the areas covered by the study, based on pre-pilot figures showing the discontinuance rates for a one month period before the schemes came into operation.

The evaluation of two of the three new schemes shows a similar increase in the discontinuance rate in the areas based on the pre-pilot figures. Prior to the introduction of PICA in Coventry eight per cent of cases were dropped compared to 11 per cent of cases where the defendant was registered for the scheme but not interviewed. In Oldham, nine per cent of cases where the defendant was not interviewed were dropped compared to just two per cent of cases in the month before the scheme was introduced. In Newcastle there was little difference in the rates at which cases were dropped prior to PICA compared to cases where the defendant was not interviewed: 12 per cent of cases were dropped in the month prior to the scheme being introduced compared to 13 per

---

[2] Data from Crown Prosecution Service performance indicators, April-June 1992
[3] Home Office Statistical Bulletin 22/93
[4] In all cases where a PICA report was prepared, it was sent to the CPS prior to first court in 90 per cent of cases in ILPS, 74 per cent in Coventry, 90 per cent in Oldham and 50 per cent in Newcastle.

cent for those registered for PICA but not interviewed.

In order for the schemes to cover their costs, much higher discontinuance rates would be required. For example, for the ILPS scheme to have covered its costs it would have needed to achieve an additional 63 public interest discontinuances - equal to almost half the cases where a report was written. In Coventry a further 101 cases would have had to be dropped, which would amount to almost all (97 per cent) cases where a report was written. Alternatively, the schemes would have to deal with a much greater volume of cases than proved possible in the pilots, but that might be difficult without drawing in more cases where the prospects of discontinuance were low.

The estimates given in this chapter cannot be regarded as more than a rough guide to the financial costs and benefits of the PICA pilot schemes. Since not all the costs and benefits can be quantified with the information currently available the figures should not be considered as providing more than a rough approximation. However, it can be concluded with some confidence that the schemes can only be run in their current form at a very substantial net cost.

# PUBLIC INTEREST CASE ASSESSMENT SCHEMES

# 5 Discussion

The schemes demonstrated that the more comprehensive information which PICA provided for the CPS meant that cases were less likely to proceed to court where this was judged to be not in the public interest. The crown prosecutors involved in the schemes were in no doubt that PICA had contributed to the quality of their decision-making. Whilst this was the central objective of PICA, it was not the sole aim. In many cases the probation service's intervention enabled them to tackle other problems with defendants which were revealed in the PICA interviews, whether or not a report was submitted. Where cases did proceed to court the CPS still found the information helpful in many instances, by providing a more informed basis for their decisions.

Against these benefits must be set the costs of the schemes, as set out in Chapter 4. In these pilot projects the savings arising from diverting cases from court fell a long way short of covering the cost of PICA in any of the areas. Even in London, which covered a higher proportion of estimated costs than other areas, it was estimated to have covered little more than a quarter of its costs. The way the schemes were set up did make a difference, and Inner London's greater experience no doubt contributed to its comparative success. The one judged least cost-effective (Newcastle) was also the one seen as having the least effective administrative arrangements. (The probation service in Northumbria recognised the problems, and substantial reorganisation of its pre-trial activities as a whole was undertaken after the evaluation was completed.)

The findings pose three central questions:

- Could the information which PICA provides be made available in any other way?
- Is it worth extending PICA to other parts of the country even if they incur substantial net costs for the criminal justice system?
- If new schemes were to be set up, what lessons should be taken on board from the pilot schemes?

**Could the information be provided in other ways?**

The police are, inevitably, the main source of information bearing on prosecution, and already screen out a substantial number of minor cases through cautioning and informal warnings. It is not realistic to expect them to have all relevant personal information, such as that relating to physical or mental health, which may be relevant to prosecution decisions. Most crown prosecutors felt that the probation service was best placed to provide the kind of information yielded by PICA. As one prosecutor commented, expressing the majority view:

# PUBLIC INTEREST CASE ASSESSMENT SCHEMES

*"It is not just a question of sitting down and filling in a form – I could do that, but I don't have the training to draw out the information that is relevant."*

However, not all probation officers felt that they alone could provide the information:

*"Social work skills in their full range are not required – just the basics of communication skills, good level of assessment and interviewing skills."*

In practice, the CPS do not get personal information about defendants from other sources very often. Occasionally defence solicitors get it touch and may provide information on, for example, the physical or mental health of the defendant. Such information is unlikely to be available as early in proceedings as that from the probation service and, of course, there are many cases in which no solicitor is employed. The probation service could itself provide information on cases where the defendant is already known to them, and occasionally does so. However, in the majority of cases those dealt with in the PICA schemes were not the kinds of defendants whom probation officers would normally have been involved with. Among other sources, crown prosecutors mentioned that on occasions defendants' families contacted them with relevant details. If ways could be found of making more widely known the kinds of factors relevant to prosecution decisions, and how to bring relevant information to the attention of those taking the decisions, this could perhaps provide some of the benefits of PICA without the costs. For example it was found in the course of PICA interviews that defendants were frequently unsure, about the criminal process. This particularly applied to first offenders. It might be possible to provide information, perhaps in the form of a leaflet, at the point of arrest about the CPS review of the case, how to obtain legal advice and the procedure if the case does go to court. It could also explain what information is relevant to the CPS decision to prosecute.

**Is it worth extending PICA?**

PICA had widespread support among prosecutors interviewed, who appreciated the additional, verified information which they did not normally get from other sources. Since PICA enabled crown prosecutors to do their job better its extension would be very much welcomed. However, it is unrealistic to imagine that the high cost of PICA will be seen as justifiable. A possible way forward would be to secure some of the benefits of PICA through other pre-trial initiatives in which the probation service is involved such as bail information schemes (see Lloyd, 1992), duty psychiatrist schemes (Joseph, 1992), panel assessment schemes for mentally disordered offenders (Hedderman, 1993) and juvenile bureaux. A review of pre-trial services to see how the various schemes could best complement one another offers a possible way forward. The results – for example, in relation to early identification of the mentally disordered – would be of value to all concerned with case processing, whether or not the case was dropped.

# DISCUSSION

**What are the lessons for any new schemes?**

If PICA were to be considered worthwhile despite the costs, the study suggests a number of factors that could usefully be taken into account.

i. There is a case for focusing more on the offender, less on the offence. A point made in interviews was that there is no obvious logic in ruling cases out of PICA simply because of the type of offence, rather that seriousness, when cautioning would not be precluded on these grounds alone.

ii. Although some cases that were discontinued were not obvious candidates for discontinuance prior to the interview, there are characteristics which make it unlikely that a case will be dropped (recent convictions for similar offences is one) and it would be desirable to draw up a more exhaustive list of criteria to target cases.

iii. It is important to recognise that defendants approached may be confused by the scheme, and be unfamiliar with the criminal process. It is essential that any scheme is explained very clearly. It would seem from the pilots that there is a need to encourage young offenders to respond, since they may be particularly strong candidates for discontinuance given the fact that the youth of the defendant is one of the public interest criteria listed in the Code.

**Conclusions**

Although the calculations are based on imperfect information there can be no doubt that, as constituted in the experiments, the PICA schemes cost a great deal more than they saved even though the rate of discontinuance where a report was prepared was substantially higher than where there was no report. In such cases they do have, however, a less quantifiable contribution to the quality of decision-making by ensuring that people are not prosecuted inappropriately. The pilot projects have identified the kind of information which would help prosecutors screen cases more effectively. Incorporation of elements of PICA into other schemes, such as those concerned with identifying mentally disordered offenders, may prove worthwhile.

PUBLIC INTEREST CASE ASSESSMENT SCHEMES

# Appendix A

**Nationally agreed inclusion and exclusion lists**

**Group A: Included Offences**

Theft (Section I of the Theft Act 1968)

Obtaining services by deception (Section 1 Theft Act 1978)

Making off with payment (Section 3 Theft Act 1978)

Removal of articles from public places (Section II Theft Act 1968)

Taking a conveyance without consent (Section 12 The Theft Act 1968)

Abstracting electricity (Section 12 Theft Act 1968)

Obtaining property by deception (Section 15 Theft Act 1968)

Obtaining pecuniary advantage by deception (Section 16 Theft Act 1968)

Evasion of liability by deception (Section 2 Theft Act 1978)

Evasion of liability by deception (Section 2 Theft Act 1978)

Dishonest handling (Section 22 Theft Act 1968)

Going equipped for theft (Section 25 Theft Act 1968)

All criminal damage (Criminal Damage Act 1971)

Drunk & disorderly (Section 91(1) Criminal Justice Act 1967)

Attempts to commit any of the above offences

**Group B: Excluded Offences**

All homicide

Death by reckless driving

All sexual offences

Burglary (Section 9 Theft Act 1968)

Aggravated burglary (Section 10 Theft Act 1968)

Robbery (Section 8 Theft Act 1968)

## PUBLIC INTEREST CASE ASSESSMENT SCHEMES

Theft from person (Section 8 Theft Act 1968)

Driving with excess alcohol

Driving whilst disqualified

Possession of Class A drug

Possession of Glass A drug with intent

Kidnapping

Blackmail

All assaults (Offences Against the Person Act 1861)

Possession of offensive weapon

Riot/Violent Disorder/Affray (Sections 1, 2, 3 of POA 1986)

Attempts to commit any of the above offences

Plus those defendants who stand to be in breach of bail or a suspended sentence

# Appendix B

**Examples of PICA reports from the pilot areas**

**Case 1**: *Offences charged: P.O.A - section 5*

**Details**. Mr A is a retired man living with his wife and son in the family home. He is dependent upon the state pension and a small pension of £12.00 per month. Mr A is in good health, although he appears rather frail.

A man of limited means and modest habits, Mr A normally only goes out of his home on Sunday lunch when his wife gives him sufficient spending money for a few drinks. On [date] he says he went to [public house] because they had a special offer of reduced price drinks. As such he was apparently able to obtain considerably more than his usual quantity of alcohol for the same money, with the consequence that he failed to maintain his usual sober state.

Mr A is proud of a good employment history and a previously unblemished record. In interview he was worried and concerned that this may now be spoilt after all these years. He is also most anxious about appearing before the court, having never attended before and being unable to afford the cost of legal representation. Mr A's circumstances, his normal drinking habits and his anxieties were confirmed by his son. I have contacted the public house visited by Mr A, and confirmed that drinks were half price on [date].

**Case 2**: *Offences charged: Theft - shoplifting*

**Details**. Mr B is a single man, divorced five years ago, who until April of this year lived alone. He is unemployed, having been made redundant in June of last year, and is dependant upon Income Support of £84.00 per two weeks. In April of this year his fifteen-year-old daughter came to live with him, being beyond the control of her mother. This has radically changed the well ordered life which Mr B had established. His daughter is said to associate with known drug users and to abuse drugs herself. To support this habit she steals from her father and his home. In his efforts to stop this, Mr B has been threatened by his daughter's associates and problems have arisen with his neighbours as a result of her behaviour. He has reported the matter to the police. As a result of his daughter's thefts he is now in arrears with his rent and, on the occasion of the offence, had no money for food.

In interview I found Mr B very distressed, so much so that I advise him to see his doctor. He feels he cannot cope with the situation. He plans to ask the local authority for a new tenancy away from his present location, and he is determined not to take his daughter with him. He has been actively seeking employment and, in response to a

# PUBLIC INTEREST CASE ASSESSMENT SCHEMES

recent application, has been informed that work in a warehouse may soon be available to him. Mr B is worried that the good record he has established over the past thirteen years may be destroyed by a conviction and diminish his employment prospects.

I have seen details of Mr B's income support and his rent book which shows arrears building up from April of this year. As Mr B had not previously consulted his doctor, I could not seek verification of his obvious stress from the source. I have, however, spoken to a neighbour - Ms Z who has known him for the past year. She confirms the stress Mr B has been subjected to since April, and how from a quiet and well respected neighbour he has now found himself in conflict with people living nearby.

**Case 3**: *Offences charged: Criminal Damage*

**Details**. In preparing this report, I have interviewed Mr C in my office. I have also received a medical certificate (copy attached) from Dr Y, his GP.

Mr C has been involved in a long standing dispute with his brother over business deals. Mr C describes how this has depressed him and he has been receiving treatment for some time now, the diagnosis being reactive depression and anxiety. There has been a psychiatric referral, and treatment has been by way of anti-depressant medication prescribed by his GP. Mr C spoke to me of occasional suicide feelings, and he does seem to be quite seriously stressed. In interview, he seemed quite depressed and I thought that on occasion, he was close to tears.

He was badly beaten up in June last year, suffering seven fractured ribs and spending eight weeks in hospital. He is still receiving follow-up treatment as a result.

I note from the prosecution report that he offered to arrange for the window to be repaired, and he says that he did turn up at the house three days after the incident with a glazier, but the window had already been repaired.

**Case 4**: *Offences charged: Theft – employer*

**Details**. Documents re: College course, educational qualifications, former employment, benefit application.

This report is based on one interview with the defendant coupled with sight of documents relating to the above.

Mr D is a single person currently residing at home with his parents and elder brother and sister. The defendant left school aged 16 in 1990 with 5 G.C.S.E passes. He then attended [college] where he subsequently completed his City and Guilds Part 1 in recreation and leisure. The defendant subsequently obtained part-time employment with [employer] and remained with them until this current matter. He has however continued with his studies and is currently attending [college] where he is on the AAT Foundation Core course in accounts. Mr D stated that he intends to study accountancy as his chosen

# APPENDIX B

career. The current course is 18 hours per week and does not attract a grant. The defendant has lost his employment as a result of the current matter and has subsequently registered for benefit. His interview with the DSS is [date] and he is consequently without means until he receives his first payment.

Mr D is aware of the possible effect a conviction for dishonesty could have on his career but intends to stay with the course.

**Case 5**: *Offences charged: Theft - shoplifting*

**Details**. This report is based on one interview held with the defendant at my office coupled with a telephone conversation with her GP.

Mrs E is a married person currently living with her husband who is now retired. Mrs E was extremely distressed and tearful during the course of the interview. She told me that her husband is now confined to the home and they survive primarily on his pension .... She informed me that she had seen her GP the day after the current incident, and had been prescribed medication to help her sleep. I subsequently contacted her GP who confirmed that the defendant has been a patient of the practice since [date] this year. She verified that Mrs E had seen her partner in August where she was first diagnosed as suffering from depression. Dr X also confirmed that as a result of her seeing the defendant she prescribed her anti-depressants to help her sleep. Dr X's opinion is that her depression and stress is connected to the difficulties Mrs E has had to shoulder in relation to her husband's condition. It is Dr X's intention to now refer Mrs E to one of their attached social workers for counselling when she sees the defendant. It was Dr X's opinion that continuation of the current proceedings would not assist this form of treatment.

**Case 6**: *Offences charged: Drunk and Disorderly*

**Details**. Mrs F lives in detached mortgaged accommodation with her husband and two children.

During an interview with Mrs F it was evident that she was in quite a state over this forthcoming appearance, she was upset and emotionally strained. Her condition was aggravated due to relationship problems, domestic pressure and her present state of health. Dr Z her doctor confirmed to me that she had known Mrs F for some time and was diagnosed as having psychological problems relating to pre menstrual tension. In the past 12 months, she had attempted suicide and had been seen by a psychiatrist, was very unstable and had come to their attention on lots of occasions due to her emotional state. Following her arrest Dr Z said she had now changed her medication and had referred her to a specialist.

Mrs F works part-time for [employer] and this was confirmed by a wage slip stating that her net pay was £579.57 per month. Mrs F said that approximately four years ago she agreed to buy her mother's council home for her. A mortgage and an Endowment policy

# PUBLIC INTEREST CASE ASSESSMENT SCHEMES

payment .. at the rate of £16.57 per month was also paid. Mrs F tells me she feels trapped by this financial commitment because it puts pressure on her to remain at work, otherwise her mother's home would be repossessed. Mrs F expressed concern over lack of personal space in her life and her tendency to turn to drink as an outlet at times of stress. The Alcohol Advisory service was discussed with her and a telephone call made to enquire about the possibility of her attending the womens group on a Wednesday evening. She was given information to enable her to make contact with them if she wished.

As a result of my concerns, I have offered Mrs F my ongoing support. I have also talked about her feelings of despair, and advised her during these times to contact the Samaritans.

**Case 7**: *Offences charged: Handling and attempted Handling*

**Details**. Mr G is a full time student at [polytechnic]. Since leaving school with six CSE qualifications and three O'levels he has continued in further education and obtained a Higher National Diploma in Engineering and completed a three months EITB approved Engineering Appreciation Workshop Certificate, all of which I had documentary evidence of. In September 1991 he was offered a place at [polytechnic] to study for a B.ENG Honours Degree in Engineering. This is normally a three year course but Mr G was given "enhanced entry" allowing him to start the course at the second year stage. He hopes to complete his studies by June 1993, then apply for sponsorship to enable him to get a Master of Science Degree in Combined Engineering.

During college vacation, in June 1991 whilst at [home] Mr G started to suffer with bad headaches, he tells me he was admitted to the [hospital] as an emergency patient, where he was diagnosed as having high blood pressure. He spent one week in hospital for observation and underwent tests. During September 1991, he was admitted into hospital again and had a kidney biopsy. He tells me that he was told that due to high blood pressure his kidneys had been damaged, and were only working at 40 per cent, less than half their capacity. Unfortunately at the time of writing this report I had not been able to verify this information, however, I was shown a letter from the medical centre stating that Mr G has regular appointments to see them with regards to his blood pressure and that they had now received the paperwork from his GP in. I was also shown a hospital appointment card confirming that Mr G had an appointment to attend [hospital] on 16 September 1991. I had evidence of his prescribed medication confirming that he was taking atenlol tablets (50mg) one daily and nifodipine (20mg) one tablet three times a day.

Whilst studying Mr G lives in student accommodation with three others. A tenancy agreement form was shown to me stating that his rent was £100 per month. Documentary evidence confirming his student grant that he received £2,364.30 per year, out of which he has to pay rent, living expenses and pay £48.26 per month to Barclays due to £1,000 student loan he took out on 10 August 1991. During the interview with Mr G he became very agitated and extremely concerned about a "conviction", and how this could affect his future employment prospects because of his intention to pursue his career in management in electrical engineering in the near future.

# Publications

The Research and Planning Unit (previously the Research Unit) has been publishing its work since 1955, and a full list of Papers is provided below. These reports are available on request from the Home Office Research and Planning Unit, Information Section, Room 278, 50 Queen Anne's Gate, London SW1H 9AT. Telephone: 071-273 2084 (answerphone).

Reports published in the HORS series are available from HMSO, who will advise as to prices, at the following address:

HMSO Publications Centre
PO Box 276
London SW8 5DT

Telephone orders: 071-873 9090

General enquiries: 071-873 0011

*Titles already published for the Home Office*

**Studies in the Causes of Delinquency and the Treatment of Offenders (SCDTO)**

1. Prediction methods in relation to borstal training. Hermann Mannheim and Leslie T. Wilkins. 1955. viii + 276pp. (11 340051 9).

2. Time spent awaiting trial. Evelyn Gibson. 1960. v + 45pp. (34-368-2)

3. Delinquent generations. Leslie T. Wilkins. 1960. iv + 20pp. (11 340053 5).

4. Murder. Evelyn Gibson and S. Klein. 1961. iv + 44pp. (11 340054 3).

5. Persistent criminals. A study of all offenders liable to preventive detention in 1956. W.H. Hammond and Edna Chayen. 1963. ix + 237pp.(34-368-5).

6. Some statistical and other numerical techniques for classifying individuals. P.McNaughton-Smith. 1965. v + 33pp. (34-368-6).

7. Probation research: a preliminary report. Part I. General outline of research. Part II. Study of Middlesex probation area (SOMPA) Steven Folkard, Kate Lyon, Margaret M. Carver and Erica O'Leary. 1966. vi + 58pp. (11 340374 7).

8. Probation research: national study of probation. Trends and regional comparisons in probation (England and Wales). Hugh Barr and Erica O'Leary. 1966. vii + 51pp. (34-368-8).

# PUBLIC INTEREST CASE ASSESSMENT SCHEMES

9. Probation research. A survey of group work in the probation service. Hugh Barr. 1966. vii + 94pp. (34-368-9).

10. Types of delinquency and home background. A validation study of Hewitt and Jenkins' hypothesis. Elizabeth Field. 1967. vi + 21pp. (34-368-10).

11. Studies of female offenders. No. 1 - Girls of 16-20 years sentenced to borstal or detention centre training in 1963. No. 2 - Women offenders in the Metropolitan Police District in March and April 1957. No. 3 - A description of women in prison on January 1, 1965. Nancy Goodman and Jean Price. 1967. v + 78pp. (34-368-11).

12. The use of the Jesness Inventory on a sample of British probationers. Martin Davies. 1967. iv + 20pp. (34-368-12).

13. The Jesness Inventory: application to approved school boys. Joy Mott. 1969. iv + 27pp. (11 340063 2).

**Home Office Research Studies (HORS)**

(Nos 1–106 are out of print)

1. Workloads in children's departments. Eleanor Grey. 1969. vi + 75pp. (11 340101 9).

2. Probationers in their social environment. A study of male probationers aged 17-20, together with an analysis of those reconvicted within twelve months. Martin Davies. 1969. vii + 204pp. (11 340102 7).

3. Murder 1957 to 1968. A Home Office Statistical Division report on murder in England and Wales. Evelyn Gibson and S. Klein (with annex by the Scottish Home and Health Department on murder in Scotland). 1969. vi + 94pp. (11 340103 5).

4. Firearms in crime. A Home Office Statistical Division report on indictable offences involving firearms in England and Wales. A. D. Weatherhead and B. M. Robinson. 1970. viii + 39pp. (11 340104 3).

5. Financial penalties and probation. Martin Davies. 1970. vii + 39pp. (11 340105 1).

6. Hostels for probationers. A study of the aims, working and variations in effectiveness of male probation hostels with special reference to the influence of the environment on delinquency. Ian Sinclair. 1971. x + 200pp. (11 340106 X).

7. Prediction methods in criminology - including a prediction study of young men on probation. Frances H. Simon. 1971. xi + 234pp.(11 340107 8).

8. Study of the juvenile liaison scheme in West Ham 1961-65. Marilyn Taylor. 1971. vi + 46pp. (11 340108 6).

9. Explorations in after-care. I - After-care units in London, Liverpool and Manchester. Martin Silberman (Royal London Prisoners' Aid Society) and Brenda Chapman.

# PUBLICATIONS

II - After-care hostels receiving a Home Office grant. Ian Sinclair and David Snow (HORU). III - St. Martin of Tours House, Aryeh Leissner (National Bureau for Co-operation in Child Care). 1971. xi + 140pp. (11 340109 4).

10. A survey of adoption in Great Britain. Eleanor Grey in collaboration with Ronald M. Blunden. 1971. ix + 168pp. (11 340110 8).

11. Thirteen-year-old approved school boys in 1960s. Elizabeth Field, W. H. Hammond and J. Tizard. 1971.ix + 46pp. (11 340111 6).

12. Absconding from approved schools. R. V. G. Clarke and D. N. Martin. 1971. vi + 146pp. (11 340112 4).

13. An experiment in personality assessment of young men remanded in custody. H. Sylvia Anthony. 1972. viii + 79pp. (11 340113 2).

14. Girl offenders aged 17-20 years. I - Statistics relating to girl offenders aged 17-20 years from 1960 to 1970. II - Re-offending by girls released from borstal or detention centre training. III - The problems of girls released from borstal training during their period on after-care. Jean Davies and Nancy Goodman. 1972. v + 77pp. (11 340114 0).

15. The controlled trial in institutional research - paradigm or pitfall for penal evaluators? R. V. G. Clarke and D. B. Cornish. 1972. v + 33pp. (11 340115 9).

16. A survey of fine enforcement. Paul Softley. 1973. v + 65pp. (11 340116 7).

17. An index of social environment - designed for use in social work research. Martin Davies. 1973. vi + 63pp. (11 340117 5).

18. Social enquiry reports and the probation service. Martin Davies and Andrea Knopf. 1973. v + 49pp.(11 340118 3).

19. Depression, psychopathic personality and attempted suicide in a borstal sample. H. Sylvia Anthony.1973. viii + 44pp. (0 11 340119 1).

20. The use of bail and custody by London magistrates' courts before and after the Criminal Justice Act 1967. Frances Simon and Mollie Weatheritt. 1974. vi + 78pp. (0 11 340120 5).

21. Social work in the environment A study of one aspect of probation practice. Martin Davies, with Margaret Rayfield, Alaster Calder and Tony Fowles. 1974. ix + 151pp. (0 11 340121 3).

22. Social work in prison. An experiment in the use of extended contact with offenders. Margaret Shaw.1974. viii + 154pp. (0 11 340122 1).

23. Delinquency amongst opiate users. Joy Mott and Marilyn Taylor. 1974. vi + 31pp. (0 11 340663 0).

# PUBLIC INTEREST CASE ASSESSMENT SCHEMES

24. IMPACT. Intensive matched probation and after-care treatment. Vol. I - The design of the probation experiment and an interim evaluation. M. S. Folkard, A. J. Fowles, B.C. McWilliams, W. McWilliams, D. D. Smith, D. E. Smith and G. R. Walmsley. 1974. v + 54pp. (0 11 340664 9).

25. The approved school experience. An account of boys' experiences of training under differing regimes of approved schools, with an attempt to evaluate the effectiveness of that training. Anne B. Dunlop. 1974. vii + l24pp. (0 11 340665 7).

26. Absconding from open prisons. Charlotte Banks, Patricia Mayhew and R. J. Sapsford. 1975. viii + 89pp. (0 11 340666 5).

27. Driving while disqualified. Sue Kriefman. 1975. vi + 136pp.(0 11 340667 3).

28. Some male offenders' problems. - Homeless offenders in Liverpool. W. McWilliams. II - Casework with short-term prisoners. Julie Holborn. 1975. x + 147pp. (0 11 340668 1).

29. Community service orders. K. Pease, P. Durkin, I. Earnshaw, D. Payne and J. Thorpe. 1975. viii + 80pp. (0 11 340669 X).

30. Field Wing Bail Hostel: the first nine months. Frances Simon and Sheena Wilson. 1975. viii + 55pp. (0 11 340670 3).

31. Homicide in England and Wales 1967-1971. Evelyn Gibson. 1975. iv + 59pp. (0 11 340753 X).

32. Residential treatment and its effects on delinquency. D. B. Cornish and R. V. G. Clarke. 1975. vi + 74pp. (0 11 340672 X).

33. Further studies of female offenders. Part A: Borstal girls eight years after release. Nancy Goodman, Elizabeth Maloney and Jean Davies. Part B: The sentencing of women at the London Higher Courts. Nancy Goodman, Paul Durkin and Janet Halton. Part C: Girls appearing before a juvenile court. Jean Davies. 1976. vi + 114pp. (0 11 340673 8).

34. Crime as opportunity. P. Mayhew, R. V. G. Clarke, A. Sturman and J. M. Hough. 1976. vii + 36pp. (0 11 340674 6).

35. The effectiveness of sentencing: a review of the literature. S. R. Brody. 1976. v + 89pp. (0 11 340675 4).

36. IMPACT. Intensive matched probation and after-care treatment. Vol. II - The results of the experiment. M. S. Folkard, D. E. Smith and D. D. Smith 1976. xi + 40pp. (0 11 340676 2).

37. Police cautioning in England and Wales. J. A. Ditchfield. 1976. v + 31pp. (0 11 340677 0).

# PUBLICATIONS

38. Parole in England and Wales. C. P. Nuttall, with E. E. Barnard, A. J. Fowles, A. Frost, W. H. Hammond, P. Mayhew, K. Pease, R. Tarling and M. J. Weatheritt. 1977. vi + 90pp. (0 11 340678 9).

39. Community service assessed in 1976. K. Pease, S. Billingham and I. Earnshaw. 1977. vi + 29pp. (0 11 340679 7).

40. Screen violence and film censorship: a review of research. Stephen Brody. 1977. vii + 179pp. (0 11 340680 0).

41. Absconding from borstals. Gloria K. Laycock. 1977. v + 82pp. (0 11 340681 9).

42. Gambling: a review of the literature and its implications for policy and research. D. B. Cornish. 1978. xii + 284pp. (0 11 340682 7).

43. Compensation orders in magistrates' courts. Paul Softley. 1978. v + 41pp. (0 11 340683 5).

44. Research in criminal justice. John Croft. 1978. iv + 16pp. (0 11 340684 3).

45. Prison welfare: an account of an experiment at Liverpool. A. J. Fowles. 1978. v + 34pp. (0 11 340685 1).

46. Fines in magistrates' courts. Paul Softley. 1978. v + 42pp. (0 11 340686 X).

47. Tackling vandalism. R. V. Clarke (editor), F. J. Gladstone, A. Sturman and Sheena Wilson 1978. vi + 91pp. (0 11 340687 8).

48. Social inquiry reports: a survey. Jennifer Thorpe. 1979. vi + 55pp. (0 11 340688 6).

49. Crime in public view. P. Mayhew, R. V. G. Clarke, J. N. Burrows, J. M. Hough and S. W. C. Winchester. 1979. v + 36pp. (0 11 340689 4).

50. Crime and the community. John Croft. 1979. v + 16pp. (0 11 340690 8).

51. Life-sentence prisoners. David Smith (editor), Christopher Brown, Joan Worth, Roger Sapsford and Charlotte Banks (contributors). 1979. iv + 51pp. (0 11 340691 6).

52. Hostels for offenders. Jane E. Andrews, with an appendix by Bill Sheppard. 1979. v + 30pp. (0 11 340692 4).

53. Previous convictions, sentence and reconviction: a statistical study of a sample of 5,000 offenders convicted in January 1971. G. J. O. Phillpotts and L. B. Lancucki. 1979. v + 55pp. (0 11 340693 2).

54. Sexual offences, consent and sentencing. Roy Walmsley and Karen White. 1979. vi + 77pp.(0 11 340694 0).

55. Crime prevention and the police. John Burrows, Paul Ekblom and Kevin Heal. 1979. v + 37pp. (0 11 340695 9).

# PUBLIC INTEREST CASE ASSESSMENT SCHEMES

56. Sentencing practice in magistrates' courts. Roger Tarling, with the assistance of Mollie Weatheritt. 1979. vii + 54pp. (0 11 340696 7).

57. Crime and comparative research. John Croft. 1979. iv + 16pp. (0 11 340697 5).

58. Race, crime and arrests. Philip Stevens and Carole F. Willis. 1979. v + 69pp. (0 11 340698 3).

59. Research and criminal policy. John Croft. 1980. iv + 14pp. (0 11 340699 1).

60. Junior attendance centres. Anne B. Dunlop. 1980. v + 47pp. (0 11 340700 9).

61. Police interrogation: an observational study in four police stations. Paul Softley, with the assistance of David Brown, Bob Forde, George Mair and David Moxon. 1980. vii + 67pp. (0 11 340701 7).

62. Co-ordinating crime prevention efforts. F. J. Gladstone. 1980. v + 74pp. (0 11 340702 5).

63. Crime prevention publicity: an assessment. D. Riley and P. Mayhew. 1980. v + 47pp. (0 11 340703 3).

64. Taking offenders out of circulation. Stephen Brody and Roger Tarling. 1980. v + 46pp. (0 11 340704 1).

65. Alcoholism and social policy: are we on the right lines? Mary Tuck. 1980. v + 30pp. (0 11 340705 X).

66. Persistent petty offenders. Suzan Fairhead. 1981. vi + 78pp. (0 11 340706 8).

67. Crime control and the police. Pauline Morris and Kevin Heal. 1981. v + 71pp. (0 11 340707 6).

68. Ethnic minorities in Britain: a study of trends in their position since 1961. Simon Field, George Mair, Tom Rees and Philip Stevens. 1981. v + 48pp. (0 11 340708 4).

69. Managing criminological research. John Croft. 1981. iv + 17pp. (0 11 340709 2).

70. Ethnic minorities, crime and policing: a survey of the experiences of West Indians and whites. Mary Tuck and Peter Southgate. 1981. iv + 54pp. (0 11 340765 3).

71. Contested trials in magistrates' courts. Julie Vennard. 1982. v + 32pp. (0 11 340766 1).

72 Public disorder: a review of research and a study in one inner city area. Simon Field and Peter Southgate. 1982. v + 77pp. (0 11 340767 X).

73. Clearing up crime. John Burrows and Roger Tarling. 1982. vii + 31pp. (0 11 340768 8).

74. Residential burglary: the limits of prevention. Stuart Winchester and Hilary Jackson. 1982. v + 47pp. (0 11 340769 6).

# PUBLICATIONS

75. Concerning crime. John Croft. 1982. iv + 16pp. (0 11 340770 X).

76. The British Crime Survey: first report. Mike Hough and Pat Mayhew. 1983. v + 62pp. (0 11 340786 6).

77. Contacts between police and public: findings from the British Crime Survey. Peter Southgate and Paul Ekblom. 1984. v + 42pp. (0 11 340771 8).

78. Fear of crime in England and Wales. Michael Maxfield. 1984. v + 57pp. (0 11 340772 6).

79. Crime and police effectiveness. Ronald V. Clarke and Mike Hough 1984. iv + 33pp. (0 11 340773 3).

80. The attitudes of ethnic minorities. Simon Field. 1984. v + 49pp. (0 11 340774 2).

81. Victims of crime: the dimensions of risk. Michael Gottfredson. 1984. v + 54pp. (0 11 340775 0).

82. The tape recording of police interviews with suspects: an interim report. Carole Willis. 1984. v + 45pp. (0 11 340776 9).

83. Parental supervision and juvenile delinquency. David Riley and Margaret Shaw. 1985. v + 90pp. (0 11 340799 8).

84. Adult prisons and prisoners in England and Wales 1970-1982: a review of the findings of social research. Joy Mott. 1985. vi + 73pp. (0 11 340801 3).

85. Taking account of crime: key findings from the 1984 British Crime Survey. Mike Hough and Pat Mayhew. 1985. vi + 115pp. (0 11 341810 2).

86. Implementing crime prevention measures. Tim Hope. 1985. vi + 82pp. (0 11 340812 9).

87. Resettling refugees: the lessons of research. Simon Field. 1985. vi + 66pp. (0 11 340815 3).

88. Investigating burglary: the measurement of police performance. John Burrows. 1986. vi + 36pp. (0 11 340824 2)

89. Personal violence. Roy Walmsley. 1986. vi + 87pp. (0 11 340827 7).

90. Police-public encounters. Peter Southgate. 1986. vi + 150pp. (0 11 340834 X).

91. Grievance procedures in prisons. John Ditchfield and Claire Austin. 1986. vi + 87pp. (0 11 340839 0).

92. The effectiveness of the Forensic Science Service. Malcolm Ramsay. 1987. v + 100pp. (0 11 340842 0).

93. The police complaints procedure: a survey of complainants' views. David Brown. 1987. v + 98pp. (0 11 340853 6).

# PUBLIC INTEREST CASE ASSESSMENT SCHEMES

94. The validity of the reconviction prediction score. Denis Ward. 1987. vi + 46. (0 11 340882 X).

95. Economic aspects of the illicit drug market enforcement policies in the United Kingdom. Adam Wagstaff and Alan Maynard. 1988. vii + 156pp. (0 11 340883 8)

96. Schools, disruptive behaviour and deliquency: a review of literature. John Graham. 1988. v + 70pp. (0 11 340887 0).

97. The tape recording of police interviews with suspects: a second interim report. Carole Willis, John Macleod and Peter Naish. 1988. vii + 97pp. (011 340890 0).

98. Triable-either-way cases: Crown Court or magistrate's court. David Riley and Julie Vennard. 1988. v + 52pp. (0 11 340891 9).

99. Directing patrol work: a study of uniformed policing. John Burrows and Helen Lewis. 1988 v + 66pp. (0 11 340891 9)

100. Probation day centres. George Mair. 1988. v + 44pp. (0 11 340894 3).

101. Amusement machines: dependency and delinquency. John Graham. 1988. v + 48pp. (0 11 340895 1).

102. The use and enforcement of compensation orders in magistrates' courts. Tim Newburn. 1988. v + 49pp. (0 11 340 896 X)

103. Sentencing practice in the Crown Court. David Moxon. 1988. v + 90pp. (0 11 340902 8).

104. Detention at the police station under the Police and Criminal Evidence Act 1984. David Brown. 1988. v + 88pp. (0 11340908 7).

105. Changes in rape offences and sentencing. Charles Lloyd and Roy Walmsley. 1989. vi + 53pp. (0 11 340910 9).

106. Concerns about rape. Lorna Smith. 1989. v + 48pp. (0 11 340911 7).

107. Domestic violence. Lorna Smith. 1989. v + 132pp. (0 11 340925 7)

108. Drinking and disorder: a study of non-metropolitan violence. Mary Tuck. 1989. v + 111pp. (011 340926 5).

109. Special security units. Roy Walmsley. 1989. v + 114pp. (0 11 340961 3).

110. Pre-trial delay: the implications of time limits. Patricia Morgan and Julie Vennard. 1989. v + 66pp. (0 11 340964 8)

111. The 1988 British Crime Survey. Pat Mayhew, David Elliott and Lizanne Dowds. 1989. v + 133pp. (0 11 340965 6).

112. The settlement of claims at the Criminal Injuries Compensation Board. Tim Newburn. 1989. v + 40pp. (0 11 340967 2).

# PUBLICATIONS

113. Race, community groups and service delivery. Hilary Jackson and Simon Field. 1989. v + 62pp. (0 11 340972 9).

114. Money payment supervision orders: probation policy and practice. George Mair and Charles Lloyd. 1989.v + 40pp. (0 11 340971 0).

115. Suicide and self-injury in prison: a literature review. Charles Lloyd. 1990. v + 69pp. (0 11 3409745 5).

116. Keeping in Touch: police-victim communication in two areas. Tim Newburn and Susan Merry. 1990. v + 52pp. (0 11 340974 5).

117. The police and public in England and Wales: a British Crime Survey report. Wesley G. Skogan. 1990. vi + 74pp. (0 11 340995 8).

118. Control in prisons: a review of the literature. John Ditchfield. 1990 (0 11 340996 6).

119. Trends in crime and their interpretation: a study of recorded crime in post-war England and Wales. Simon Field. 1990. (0 11 340994 X).

120. Electronic monitoring: the trials and their results. George Mair and Claire Nee. 1990. v + 79pp. (0 11 340998 2).

121. Drink driving: the effects of enforcement. David Riley. 1991. viii + 78pp. (0 11 340999 0).

122. Managing difficult prisoners: the Parkhurst Special Unit. Roy Walmsley (Ed.) 1991. x + 139pp (0 11 341008 5).

123. Investigating burglary: the effects of PACE. David Brown. 1991. xii + 106pp. (0 11 341011 5).

124. Traffic policing in changing times. Peter Southgate and Catriona Mirrlees-Black. 1991. viii + 139pp (0 11 341019 0)

125. Magistrates' court or Crown Court ? Mode of trial decisions and sentencing. Carol Hedderman and David Moxon. 1992. vii + 53pp. (0 11 341036 0).

126. Developments in the use of compensation orders in magistrates' courts since October 1988. David Moxon, John Martin Corkery and Carol Hedderman. 1992. x + 48pp. (0 11 341042 5).

127. A comparative study of firefighting arrangements in Britain, Denmark, the Netherlands and Sweden. John Graham, Simon Field, Roger Tarling and Heather Wilkinson. 1992. x + 57pp. (0 11 341043 3).

128. The National Prison Survey 1991: main findings. Roy Walmsley, Liz Howard and Sheila White. 1992. xiv + 82pp. (0 11 341051 4).

129. Changing the Code: police detention under the revised PACE Codes of Practice. David Brown, Tom Ellis and Karen Larcombe. 1992. viii + 122pp. (0 11 341052 2).

# PUBLIC INTEREST CASE ASSESSMENT SCHEMES

130. Car theft: the offender's perspective. Roy Light, Claire Nee and Helen Ingham. 1993. x + 89pp. (0 11 341069 7).

131. Housing, Community and Crime: The Impact of the Priority Estates Project. Janet Foster and Timothy Hope with assistance from Lizanne Dowds and Mike Sutton. 1993. xi + 118. (0 11 341078 6).

132. The 1992 British Crime Survey. Pat Mayhew, Natalie Aye Maung and Catriona Mirrlees-Black. 1993. xiii + 206. ( 0 11 341094 8).

**Research and Planning Unit Papers (RPUP)**

1. Uniformed police work and management technology. J. M. Hough. 1980.

2. Supplementary information on sexual offences and sentencing. Roy Walmsley and Karen White. 1980.

3. Board of visitor adjudications. David Smith, Claire Austin and John Ditchfield. 1981.

4. Day centres and probation. Suzan Fairhead, with the assistance of J.Wilkinson-Grey. 1981.

5. Ethnic minorities and complaints against the police. Philip Stevens and Carole Willis. 1982.

6. Crime and public housing. Mike Hough and Pat Mayhew (editors). 1982.

7. Abstracts of race relations research. George Mair and Philip Stevens (editors). 1982.

8. Police probationer training in race relations. Peter Southgate. 1982.

9. The police response to calls from the public. Paul Ekblom and Kevin Heal. 1982.

10. City centre crime: a situational approach to prevention. Malcolm Ramsay. 1982.

11. Burglary in schools: the prospects for prevention. Tim Hope. 1982.

12. Fine enforcement. Paul Softley and David Moxon. 1982.

13. Vietnamese refugees. Peter Jones. 1982.

14. Community resources for victims of crime. Karen Williams. 1983.

15. The use, effectiveness and impact of police stop and search powers. Carole Willis. 1983.

16. Acquittal rates. Sid Butler. 1983.

17. Criminal justice comparisons: the case of Scotland and England and Wales. Lorna J. F. Smith. 1983.

18. Time taken to deal with juveniles under criminal proceedings. Catherine Frankenburg and Roger Tarling. 1983.

# PUBLICATIONS

19. Civilian review of complaints against the police: a survey of the United States literature. David C. Brown. 1983.

20. Police action on motoring offences. David Riley. 1983.

21. Diverting drunks from the criminal justice system. Sue Kingsley and George Mair. 1983.

22. The staff resource implications of an independent prosecution system. Peter R. Jones. 1983.

23. Reducing the prison population: an exploratory study in Hampshire. David Smith, Bill Sheppard, George Mair, Karen Williams. 1984.

24. Criminal justice system model: magistrates' courts sub-model. Susan Rice. 1984.

25. Measures of police effectiveness and efficiency. Ian Sinclair and Clive Miller. 1984.

26. Punishment practice by prison Boards of Visitors. Susan Iles, Adrienne Connors, Chris May, Joy Mott. 1984.

27. Reparation, conciliation and mediation: current projects and plans in England and Wales. Tony Marshall. 1984.

28. Magistrates' domestic courts: new perspectives. Tony Marshall (editor). 1984.

29. Racism awareness training for the police. Peter Southgate. 1984.

30. Community constables: a study of a policing initiative. David Brown and Susan Iles. 1985.

31. Recruiting volunteers. Hilary Jackson. 1985.

32. Juvenile sentencing: is there a tariff? David Moxon, Peter Jones, Roger Tarling. 1985.

33. Bringing people together: mediation and reparation projects in Great Britain. Tony Marshall and Martin Walpole. 1985.

34. Remands in the absence of the accused. Chris May. 1985.

35. Modelling the criminal justice system. Patricia M. Morgan. 1985.

36. The criminal justice system model: the flow model. Hugh Pullinger. 1986.

37. Burglary: police actions and victim views. John Burrows. 1986.

38. Unlocking community resources: four experimental government small grants schemes. Hilary Jackson. 1986.

39. The cost of discriminating: a review of the literature. Shirley Dex. 1986.

40. Waiting for Crown Court trial: the remand population. Rachel Pearce. 1987.

# PUBLIC INTEREST CASE ASSESSMENT SCHEMES

41. Children's evidence: the need for corroboration. Carol Hedderman. 1987.

42. A prelimary study of victim offender mediation and reparation schemes in England and Wales. Gwynn Davis, Jacky Boucherat, David Watson, Adrian Thatcher (Consultant). 1987.

43. Explaining fear of crime: evidence from the 1984 British Crime Survey. Michael Maxfield. 1987.

44. Judgements of crime seriousness: evidence from the 1984 British Crime Survey. Ken Pease. 1988.

45. Waiting time on the day in magistrates' courts: a review of case listings practices. David Moxon and Roger Tarling (editors). 1988.

46. Bail and probation work: the ILPS temporary bail action project. George Mair. 1988.

47. Police work and manpower allocation. Roger Tarling. 1988.

48. Computers in the courtroom. Carol Hedderman. 1988.

49. Data interchange between magistrates' courts and other agencies. Carol Hedderman. 1988.

50. Bail and probation work II: the use of London probation/bail hostels for bailees. Helen Lewis and George Mair. 1989.

51. The role and function of police community liaison officers. Susan V. Phillips and Raymond Cochrane. 1989.

52. Insuring against burglary losses. Helen Lewis. 1989.

53. Remand decisions in Brighton and Bournemouth. Patricia Morgan and Rachel Pearce. 1989.

54. Racially motivated incidents reported to the police. Jayne Seagrave. 1989.

55. Review of research on re-offending of mentally disordered offenders. David J. Murray. 1990.

56. Risk prediction and probation: papers from a Research and Planning Unit workshop. George Mair (editor). 1990.

57. Household fires: findings from the British Crime Survey 1988. Chris May. 1990.

58. Home Office funding of victim support schemes - money well spent? Justin Russell. 1990.

59. Unit fines: experiments in four courts. David Moxon, Mike Sutton and Carol Hedderman. 1990.

# PUBLICATIONS

60. Deductions from benefit for fine default. David Moxon, Carol Hedderman and Mike Sutton. 1990.

61. Monitoring time limits on custodial remands. Paul F. Henderson. 1991.

62. Remands in custody for up to 28 days: the experiments. Paul F. Henderson and Patricia Morgan. 1991.

63. Parenthood training for young offenders: an evaluation of courses in Young Offender Institutions. Diane Caddle. 1991.

64. The multi-agency approach in practice: the North Plaistow racial harassment project. William Saulsbury and Benjamin Bowling. 1991.

65. Offending while on bail: a survey of recent studies. Patricia M. Morgan. 1992.

66. Juveniles sentenced for serious offences: a comparison of regimes in Young Offender Institutions and Local Authority Community Homes. John Ditchfield and Liza Catan. 1992.

67. The management and deployment of police armed response vehicles. Peter Southgate. 1992.

68. Using psychometric personality tests in the selection of firearms officers. Catriona Mirrlees-Black. 1992.

69. Bail information schemes: practice and effect. Charles Lloyd. 1992.

70. Crack and cocaine in England and Wales. Joy Mott (editor). 1992.

71. Rape: from recording to conviction. Sharon Grace, Charles Lloyd and Lorna J.F. Smith. 1992.

72. The National Probation Survey 1990. Chris May. 1993.

73. Public satisfaction with police services. Peter Southgate and Debbie Crisp. 1993.

74. Disqualification from driving: an effective penalty? Catriona Mirrlees-Black. 1993.

75. Detention under the Prevention of Terrorism (Temporary Provisions) Act 1989: Access to legal advice and outside contact. David Brown. 1993.

76. Panel assessment schemes for mentally disordered offenders. Carol Hedderman. 1993.

77. Cash-limiting the probation service: a case study in resource allocation. Simon Field and Mike Hough. 1993

78. The probation response to drug misuse. Claire Nee and Rae Sibbitt. 1993.

79. Approval of rifle and target shooting clubs: the effects of the new and revised criteria. John Martin Corkery. 1993.

# PUBLIC INTEREST CASE ASSESSMENT SCHEMES

80. The long-term needs of victims: A review of the literature. Tim Newburn. 1993.

81. The welfare needs of unconvicted prisoners. Diane Caddle and Sheila White. 1994.

82. Racially motivated crime: a British Crime Survey analysis. Natalie Aye Maung and Catriona Mirrlees-Black. 1994.

83. Mathematical models for forecasting Passport demand. Andy Jones and John MacLeod. 1994.

84. The theft of firearms. John Corkery. 1994.

85. Equal opportunities and the Fire Service. Tom Bucke. 1994.

**Research Findings**

(These are summaries of reports and are also available from the Information Section)

1. Magistrates' court or Crown Court? Mode of trial decisions and their impact on sentencing. Carol Hedderman and David Moxon. 1992.

2. Surveying crime: findings from the 1992 British Crime Survey. Pat Mayhew and Natalie Aye Maung. 1992.

3. Car Theft: the offenders's perspective: Claire Nee. 1993.

4. The National Prison survey 1991: main findings. Roy Walmsley, Liz Howard and Sheila White. 1993.

5. Changing the Code: Police detention under the revised PACE codes of practice. David Brown, Tom Ellis and Karen Larcombe. 1993.

6. Rifle and pistol target shooting clubs: The effects of new approval criteria. John M Corkery. 1993.

7. Self-reported drug misuse in England and Wales. Main findings from the 1992 British Crime Survey. Joy Mott and Catriona Mirrlees-Black. 1993.

8. Findings from the International Crime Survey. Pat Mayhew. 1994.

9. Fear of Crime: Findings from the 1992 British Crime Survey. Catriona Mirrlees-Black and Natalie Aye Maung. 1994.

10. Does the Criminal Justice system treat men and women differently? Carol Hedderman and Mike Hough. 1994.

11. Participation in Neighbourhood Watch: Findings from the 1992 British Crime Survey. Lizanne Dowds and Pat Mayhew. 1994.

12. Not published yet.

13. Equal opportunities and the Fire Service. Tom Bucke. 1994.

# PUBLICATIONS

14. Trends in Crime: Findings from the 1994 British Crime Survey. Pat Mayhew, Catriona Mirrlees-Black and Natalie Aye Maung. 1994.

**Research Bulletin (available from the Information Section)**

The Research Bulletin is published twice a year and consists mainly of short articles relating to projects which are part of the Home Office Research and Planning Unit's research programme.

**Occasional Papers**

**(These can be purchased from the main Home Office Library Publications Unit, 50 Queen Anne's Gate, London SWIH 9AT. Telephone 071-273 2302 for information on price and availability. Those marked with an asterisk are out of print.)**

*The 'watchdog' role of Boards of Visitors. Mike Maguire and Jon Vagg. 1984.

Shared working between Prison and Probation Officers. Norman Jepson and Kenneth Elliot. 1985.

After-care Services for Released Prisoners: A Review of the Literature. Kevin Haines. 1990.

*Arts in Prisons: towards a sense of achievement. Anne Peaker and Jill Vincent. 1990.

Pornography: impacts and influences. Dennis Howitt and Guy Cumberbatch. 1990.

*An evaluation of the live link for child witnesses. Graham Davies and Elizabeth Noon. 1991.

Mentally disordered prisoners. John Gunn, Tony Maden and Mark Swinton. 1991.

Coping with a crisis: the introduction of three and two in a cell. T. G. Weiler 1992.

Psychiatric Assessment at the Magistrates' Court. Philip Joseph. 1992.

Measurement of caseload weightings in magistrates' courts. Richard J. Gadsden and Graham J. Worsdale. 1992.

The CDE of scheduling in magistrates' courts. John W Raine and Michael J. Willson. 1992.

Employment opportunities for offenders. David Downes. 1993.

Sex offenders: a framework for the evaluation of community-based treatment. Mary Barker and Rod Morgan. 1993.

Suicide attempts and self-injury in male prisons. Alison Liebling and Helen Krarup. 1993.

Measurement of caseload weightings associated with the Children's Act. Richard J. Gadsden and Graham J. Worsdale. 1994. (available from the RPU Information Section).

# PUBLIC INTEREST CASE ASSESSMENT SCHEMES

Managing difficult prisoners: The Lincoln and Hull special units. Professor Keith Bottomley, Professor Norman Jepson, Mr Kenneth Elliott and Dr Jeremy Coid. 1994 (available from RPU Information Section).

The Nacro diversion iniative for mentally disturbed offenders: an account and an evaluation. Home Office, NACRO and Mental Health Foundation (available from Information Section).

**Other Publications by members of RPU (available from HMSO)**

Designing out crime. R. V. G. Clarke and P. Mayhew (editors). 1980. viii + 186pp. (0 11 340732 7).

Policing today. Kevin Heal, Roger Tarling and John Burrows (editors). v + 181pp. (0 11 340800 5).

Managing criminal justice: a collection of papers. David Moxon (editor). 1985. vi + 222pp. (0 11 340811 0).

Situational crime prevention: from theory into practice. Kevin Heal and Gloria Laycock (editors). 1986. vii + 166pp. (0 11 340826 9)

Communities and crime reduction. Tim Hope and Margaret Shaw (editors). 1988. vii + 311pp. (11 340892 7).

New directions in police training. Peter Southgate (editor). 1988. xi + 256pp (11 340889 7).

Crime and Accountability: Victim/Offender Mediation in Practice. Tony F Marshall and Susan Merry. 1990. xii + 262. (0 11 340973 7).

Community Work and the Probation Service. Paul Henderson and Sarah del Tufo. 1991. vi + 120. (0 11 341004 2).

Part Time Punishment? George Mair. 1991. 258 pp. (0 11 340981 8).

Analysing Offending. Data, Models and Interpretations. Roger Tarling. 1993. viii + 203. (0 11 341080 8).

# PUBLICATIONS